Squatters' Farm

Kipkeny Lagat

Published by Dolman Scott Ltd

Copyright©KipkenyLagat 2017

All rights reserved. No part of this publication may be reproduced, stored in a retrieval system, or transmitted in any form or by any means, electronic, mechanical, photocopy, recording or otherwise, without prior written permission of the copyright owner. Nor can it be circulated in any form of binding or cover other than that in which it is published and without similar condition including this condition being imposed on a subsequent purchaser

ISBN: 978-1-911412-30-4

Dolman Scott Ltd

www.dolmanscott.co.uk

Dedication

To my departed paternal grandparents, whose prowess in narrating their stories of resilience towards intricacies of life, during pre-independence and post-independence periods inspired the writing of this great story.

Acknowledgement

I tender unreserved appreciation to my book agent Dr Kibnyaanko Seroney for his unrelenting support throughout the publishing process. I do also owe deep gratitude to teacher Lilian Ogutu and teacher Patsy Spiller for dedicating time out of their busy schedules to go through the manuscript at its raw stages.

Contents

Dedication .... *iii*
Acknowledgement .... *iv*
Chapter One *1*
Chapter Two *11*
Chapter Three *21*
Chapter Four *33*
Chapter Five *41*
Chapter Six *55*
Chapter Seven *67*
Chapter Eight *76*
Chapter Nine *90*
Chapter Ten *98*
Chapter Eleven *105*
Chapter Twelve *117*
Chapter Thirteen *129*
Chapter Fourteen *137*
Chapter Fifteen *149*
Chapter Sixteen *160*
Chapter Seventeen *168*
Chapter Eighteen *175*
Chapter Nineteen *184*
Chapter Twenty *197*

Chapter One

More often than not, many cannot bear to recount in any detail the miserable histories they underwent in their youth, while at the same time managing to keep their emotions at bay, without arousing the sympathy of their readers and listeners. In my case therefore, I have tried to the utmost of my ability to avoid the same issue arising. For this reason, I have undertaken to unfold this story right from the beginning, so that my narration from the onset will not end up sounding like gobbledygook.

Before carrying on, I must point out clearly that by doing this, I am not in any particular way trying to apply for my readers' belated pity and understanding, because to me it is no longer useful and I neither need it now nor hereafter.

Everything trickles back to those salad days of my boyhood, the time when the world was still so new to me, and I had hardly started to tell the difference between the present and the past, though I had commenced to think slightly beyond my nose. This is the time it dawned on me that we were being brought up together with the rest on a pretty squatters' farm. Situated in one of the republic's fertile high tablelands -Sirwa plateau was to us the equivalent of a halcyon place, a paradise on earth. The farm's environs were vibrant with undisturbed and unpolluted rural life teeming with variety of wildlife among them giraffes and gazelles, a typical veld shrouded in mystical and breathtaking scenery, which was often claimed to have never been touched by man.

The farm was in itself a joint co-operative comprising about twenty squatter families. It was a giant tract of land whose surface area to me was equal in acreage, to put it in terms of years, to two millennia. It was the remnant of one of those renowned former White Settler Farms located in the heart of the previous and famous Afrikaans Farming District.

To the South the farm was bordered partly by Naseru railway Station and the great westbound railway line. At about two hundred metres west of the station, the railway line branched off into a raised stripe of red earth on which were laid shiny steel rails heading to Katalel. This was a prominent land in the north steeped heavily in corn and milk, and the republic's leading grain basket. This railway line gave the farmland its western boundary.

To the north, its bounds were beyond my childhood horizons. All that I knew, based on the intelligence I had gathered, was that it was going further beyond the popularly known Great Trans-African trunk road which ran through the District. The Eastern side bordered mostly onto an expansive tract of government owned land which was clearly marked with two-metre high concrete beacons that ran at intervals of about hundred metres; and partly privately-owned lands to the Southeast.

A slight description of the farmland is that it was somewhat carefully planned to accommodate extensive mixed farming activities. For instance, all the farm's quarters were situated on a line to the south adjacent to the railway station. The entire surroundings of the farm were enclosed by vast, fruitful and fertile wheat fields which were cash crops cultivated by the farm members. The cash accrued from the sale of the wheat was mostly spent on what was termed as paying instalments to the former white settler. From what I had heard at the time, possession of the land was to be officially handed over to the squatters after settling their last instalments. The wheat field was followed by another ring of maize fields equally divided between all member families, which provided a food crop mainly for subsistence. The remaining mid-part was used as a grazing field for the farm's livestock.

A brief introduction of the twenty squatter families is as follows: to the East of the line was a semi-permanent house with a roof of iron sheets and wooden walls, owned by Jackton Kipwarir- the farm's prominent, aggressive but semi-literate, left-handed headman. At the Western extreme end were two mud-walled, rounded houses with grass-thatched roofs belonging to Jethro Kiperng'eng, the farm's boastful and somewhat obsequious assistant headman. In between were the dwellings of the rest of the community members, which included my parents' two single-roomed houses, both with iron sheet roofs and walls; which was a common trend with the rest of the members. Our houses were next to the farm's assistant headman, to the west. To the East was Tiebo Songhor's family's houses – she was a perpetual drunkard and the noisiest old woman in the entire farm. She was a mother to two barbaric and chaotic school dropout sons-Josiah and Johanna - and also a grandmother to two girls, Chemaiyo and Chemtai.

Just before the farm quarters was a road that was mainly dominated by hired tractors and combine harvesters during the cultivating and harvesting seasons. It occasionally acted as a playground for farm children, mostly in the evenings after school and at weekends.

Prying more deeply into those happy bygone days, especially when I was still too young to herd, I can recall that I could not tell my dreams. Then, life to me seemed like a long way without a turn. I had no words to spell my childish fears and joys. Love, lust for life, and desire laden with insatiable curiosity seemed to sing loudly within my youthful blood. To me, everyone's life seemed to be heavy with burning desires to puzzle out the fantasies of life, without a thought of what the future had in its unknown store for us.

Chapter One

I can remember vividly that, despite my tender age, I used to suffer from wanderlust. I had itchy feet with a ceaseless desire to mooch about and roam the land together with my peers. Every morning at the break of a new day, I would gulp down cupfuls of milk, followed by a cup of tea later after sunrise, which I believed would warm up the cold milk already in my belly. As the elder people began their daily chores, which started with milking and taking the milk churns heavy with milk to the milk collection centres operated by co-operative societies, I would embark on my daily routine of roaming with my fellow farm children. Sometimes we would even leave before sheep, goats and cattle were let out of their enclosures.

We would go about the fields aimlessly, engaging in all sorts of juvenile activities. We would play hide and seek games, climbing trees, at one time racing each other excitedly, shouting and whistling funny obscene tunes. Like calves well fed with milk, we would sometimes frisk and caper in the fields, but the only difference between us and the calves was that we had no tails to raise in the air. One striking thing, however, is that despite my curiosity to discover more about the farm, I never personally reached its bounds to the North.

Like all other children, many a time we would not miss an opportunity to engage in all sorts of amusing mischief. I remember times when we would succumb to temptation and invade a greening wheat field with tender wheat crops, and start somersaulting on the soft well-tilled soils. We would even trample a large area till it lay hard and flat as an envelope. But we did such a thing when further away and out of sight of the farm quarters, because if by any chance we happened to be noticed or caught red-handed by my Grandpa, who was a custodian of the farm wheat field, for sure that evening would be our time for reckoning. We would end up being rounded up, lined up on the farm's main road, lying flat on our bellies as all our parents would spank and cane us in turns till our bottoms would ache. If by any chance our misdeeds went unnoticed on one day and be discovered later on by my Grandpa on his usual patrols, we would falsely accuse the children from the neighbouring areas, especially from Chepwirwir, which was a neighbouring village to the west, dominated by the presence of towering water-pumping windmills in which their existence dated back to the colonial period. We would even go to the extent of swearing to have seen them doing so by licking our index fingers and pointing them to the sky. This would sometimes end up by resulting in bad blood between us and the boys from that village. This enmity would once in a while degenerate into fist fights whenever we came into contact. The bone of contention was that we had made them suffer for our sins. This was because whenever we wrongly accused them, our parents led by my Grandpa would troop into the village, carrying canes in their hands to tell their parents about their supposed misdeeds, and they in turn would not hesitate to lambast their boys with the assistance of our parents who were ever ready to lend a hand.

In spite of my involvement in such activities, I was in most cases the coolest and more or less the most prudent child in the entire farm. I was known as the one without the guts to speak out or rather confess, especially in the presence of any elderly person, unless I was asked a question. It was even unbelievable to many people that I could participate in any fight or mischievous activity in common with the other farm children- thus the old woman and our immediate neighbour, Tiebo Songhor, one day while drunk had nicknamed me Kipsisei, which meant the meek and cool one. She had sung herself hoarse and danced herself lame calling out my name amid the sarcastic cheers of my mates, an event which made me love and hate her in equal measure. This name quickly spread, and came to sound like my real name, used within and without the farm.

As it is always said that he knows most who speaks least, and still waters run deep, there was something associated with my quietude and strangeness. In my silence was ecstasy and anxiety, rich and deep, unstained by words. People had not corrupted my feelings and to me, life and desire were still pure because they were always unheard. To crown it all, I seemed to be extra-observant and keen on anything going on or said within and without the farm.

For instance, there were some things that used to happen and be said that usually awakened my mind and sometimes petrified me to the extent than it seemed to amuse others. I can remember one time when there were some rumours being peddled in the air that the farm's top officials, headed by Mr.Jackton Kipwarir and his deputy Mr.Jethro Kiperng'eng, had colluded with some outsiders and formed a racket that was busy registering and incorporating some outsiders onto the squatters' list for remuneration. These allegations had aroused the farm members to take action. An urgent meeting was called. In the meeting some members suggested that it would be wise if the land was shared among the squatters so that each would contribute independently to avoid the impending issue.

What followed was hell. Even before Arap Nyongio, who was presenting the suggestion, had found words to support his argument, the air was already blue with protesting words. Jackton Kipwarir the headman jumped on his feet in vehement protest.

'Arap Nyongio, who are you to make decisions on behalf of the farm? You have no right to suggest anything.' The headman glared menacingly with his staff in his left hand ready to strike.

'We cannot commit the taboo of preparing milk gourds before the cow has fully calved down,'Kiperng'eng, the assistant head, seconded in protest.

'Those are words that come from the brain and not the head like those uttered by Arap Nyongio,' Arap Magaetei, another aging member, had added, backing up the heads. There were rumours that he was also among the brokers broking with the outsiders.

Chapter One

In a minute, pandemonium reigned in the meeting, forcing some members to walk out, and the meeting was suspended indefinitely. From a safe distance where we had sat witnessing the episode of the elderly verbal strife, we could see everyone walking out one by one, and others in twos and threes with dismissive gestures.

Kipwarir was the last one to leave, after his deputy Kiperng'eng, arguing with himself all the way to his house in a soliloquy. He swayed and wielded his staff, which was his common companion, from left to right contemptuously. Many a time we had heard that crossing his path during such moments, was like asking for a thorough beating with his walking stick as he released his pent-up anger on you. For some time, he kept on arguing, once in a while stopping, turning back and hurling one or two insults at nobody. Without mincing words, he was a most tempestuous and morose person, but some said that this could be attributed to his illiteracy. I recall that sometimes he would go on yelling for some hours till filthy white froth appeared at the corners of his mouth.

This time he did not quarrel with himself much, maybe because it was already past lunchtime and the sun at its hottest peak. In front of his house, his wife Magdalena tried beseeching him to calm down and get in to have his lunch - an act which eventually bore fruit. He only muttered something like, 'Some people's heads are only masses without brains,' before he disappeared into his wooden house with a final dismissive gesture.

The atmosphere resumed its amiable ambience once more as the tension that had been caused by the pandemonium calmed down. The headman only showed up much later in the evening when he emerged from his house in his usual grayish raincoat pushing beside him his old rusty, noisy and nearly unrideable bicycle that we had nicknamed *seketa,* meaning ramshackle. He rolled it slowly along the path that joined his house to the road that ran in front of the farm quarters. Even from a distance, you could still see that he was really disturbed beyond any reason. On arriving at the road, he mounted the bicycle and cycled it furiously and meditatively downwards across the level crossing towards Chesarma shopping centre, nearly two kilometers west of the farm but slightly beyond Chepwirwir village. This was the place where most of the men in the region gathered in the evenings to booze and release their day's pent-up stress and annoyance. They enjoyed barbecued beef and mutton, sometimes dabbling in politics to discuss the day away, while others used the opportunity to patch up their differences.

Chapter Two

To anyone who has got some sense and prudence in his or her psyche, you can easily feel or tell how near or far a person is from the truth, based on how the accused reacts to an allegation. I felt that whatever had disturbed the headman and his colleagues was not something to be ignored. It was a fact, and facts are known to be very stubborn things- for they always speak for themselves.

Many a time, I had discovered that when a fly enters into a spider's territory and is slightly trapped in the cobweb, it must struggle to free itself. But sometimes, in its attempts to disentangle itself, it may end up entangling itself more - to the point of no escape and thus the spider in turn is supposed to set upon it and have his meal. Unfortunately for the spider, this does not always happen; every so often, the fly can succeed in shaking off the web and free itself because of the spider's ignorance and reluctance. Precisely, I felt, this was how Jackton

Kipwarir and his haughty colleagues managed to get through the allegations hurled at their heads, since afterwards, nobody seemed to bother or care about following up the issue.

However, it was not so long again before other rumours started loading the air once more, but this time it seemed not to carry very much weight because the source of this rumour happened to be hearsay from women gossips. Usually during certain times in the afternoons, farm women, including Mama and Kiperg'engs wife Tapsaga, would gather to tittle-tattle the afternoon away. I had discovered that they would whisper in the presence of any elderly man, speak parabolically or switch onto another topic altogether whenever a man was within earshot, but would ignore our presence, not knowing what was going through my mind --never realizing that I was not that naive like the others. By whatever means I would linger around, hanging on every word they said, since at that very tender age I had learnt that when the women utter something, it is not always so far from the truth-you can call me effeminate if you wish, but I have already spoken out my mind.

It was during such gossiping that I came across frightening rumours that left a lot to be desired in my mind. I overheard that Jackton Kipwarir, the farm headman, in conjunction with his deputy, Jethro Kiperng'eng, were surreptitiously siphoning off money from the farm's joint account, to which they were the signatories, and embezzling it. It was somehow amusing to hear that Kiperng'eng was using the money to drink and keeping his toothless concubine at Chepkinoyo; a small centre located at the outskirts of Nondoreet, our district's capital where he sometimes used to disappear for fortnights.

How the farm headman used his embezzled funds was different. Being a teetotaler, it was said that he used the money to buy meat and sugar on a daily basis. This was probably true, because every evening as he returned from Chesarma shopping centre, he would frequently be carrying two kilograms of meat and sugar each, tightly tied on the carrier of his bicycle. Consequently, his house would not miss elevenses and evening tea, something which was not that common in the homes of other member families.

Strictly and sincerely speaking, Kipwarir himself was the best tea taker and somehow addicted to it. Kipronyei, his fourth born son and my closest ally as well as my age mate, and one of the rollicking characters in the farm, used to admit it openly.

'My father is a generator that consumes tea in place of petrol,' he would say laughing foolishly. 'I imagine he clears a full twelve-cup kettle all by himself every morning and evening,' he would go on as we laughed at his outspokenness. However, to cut a long story short, none of the above allegations survived any closer investigation and all these issues were left pending since no-one else seemed bothered to probe further.

By the time all these were happening, it was approaching the evening of the year and the late year's rains were beginning to relent, giving us a dry spell that is propitious for harvesting maize and wheat, which were already beginning to turn golden in the fields, heavy with grains.

Normally this was a golden period which many always longed for. As usual people started to forget their differences, looking forward with great expectation to the approach of the end of the year. Being a high season characterized by various festivities, everyone began to wear festive looks. Every face was wreathed in smiles; moreover it is a period where everybody rolls in money, ranging from infants to the elderly, as a result of selling of the harvest. Harvesting arrangements pre-occupied the minds of the people and everyone became more engaged than ever due to the work at hand. Favourable climatic conditions had been prevalent throughout the year, and as a result, a prosperous harvest was already being predicted.

First, the maize plantations were cut and collected in stooks to dry. On the other hand, the dry eastern wind, which had started to blow across the expansive wheat fields succeeded in dispelling the moisture in the wheat crops speeding up their drying to the expected superb moisture content, making them excellently ripe for harvesting.

Every farm child, obviously including myself, started to brim over with joy, curiosity and great expectation, for all of us seemed equally attracted and captivated by machinery; especially the complexity of the combine harvesters. In general, there was a song in every heart, a smile on every face and delight in every step. Everyone seemed a lot happier than ever before.

It was not so long before the hired tractors and combine harvesters started to report to the farm premises. Normally in the yester years, they used to camp for a week but this time round it looked as if it would take longer than that, since the harvests that year were more bountiful compared to the preceding years. The convoy comprised two tractors and three combine harvesters, all of them brand new and shiny. The grapevine had it that they were owned by one of the district's leading hoity-toity magnates who lived in the outskirts of Nondoreet, our District capital. I understood that the tycoon was a close relation of His Excellency Mr. Elder Statesman, the president of our republic of Kalyaland, who, based on what I had heard, was a very big-man-in-a-higher-place beyond the reach of ordinary people and children, best known by the name – The beloved-father-of-the-nation and the commander-in-chief of a big group of fighters. At that time I had never set my eyes on him live but only heard about him, and seen his image on the currencies, and his picture preceding every telecast and his name being mentioned in every radio newscast and news brief. Funnily enough, his every movement and action, even when he went to church, formed part of the daily news. Unlike other children who used to over-adore him, I personally used to careless about him, something which my mates had warned me about, saying that if I happened to be overheard by his personal detectives, who were said to be present everywhere, I would be abducted and taken into torture chambers and underground dungeons located in Loilrobi, Kalyaland's main capital. Some people said that everyone who had been heard putting Mr. Elder Statesman's credibility into disrepute had ended up in this infamous place of no return, and those who managed to return came back half dead, something that almost instilled untold fear into my heart.

As the machinery approached the farm quarters that evening, we raced towards it with open arms in a bid to welcome them once again to our farmland, everyone cheering merrily. Those who were a bit younger and afraid of machines, especially my two younger sisters, Chebusho and Tatamei, took to their heels towards the houses and immured themselves inside screaming madly, while others, whose mothers happened to be within, sought their refuge with them. On meeting them, we turned and raced back after them on both sides singing and cheering merrily to them as they roared, purred and wailed their way towards the farm quarters, where they were parked in front of the Kipwarir's house, waiting for the next day embarkation on work in the wheat fields.

No sooner had the machines pulled up in the parking lot than more children continued to breeze in, including those from the neighbouring villages. Soon the entire place around the machines was crowded with multitudes of children all staring at the fascinating sight of the metallic giants, most of them with mouths agape. Each of us seemed teased with perplexing questions in our minds, others giving a timid bow to those sons of white men who invented and innovated such complex metallic giants, larger than their own brains.

'A human brain's size cannot match its capacity,' I heard Kipwarir's elder son Kibelat exclaiming, amid other older farm boys including Kiptolo, my elder brother. Both were in the upper classes and probably knew more than the rest of us.

'Yes,' admitted my elder brother gesturing at the enormous combine harvester towering high above us.

'Imagine - all these powerful, weighty and huge metallic giants are nothing more than the children of man's brain.' By this time others were busy reflecting their images on the machines' shiny bodies and headlights, some trying to explain how they worked and trying to convince others to believe in their words.

We lingered around the parked combine harvesters and tractors for a long time until we were reminded that dusk was encroaching and we were supposed to lead the cattle and goats into their enclosures. Some that evening were even reminded to take their evening meals but they seemed not to take heed, not until Kipwarir emerged and dispersed them with a cane, making everyone flee at top speed to their respective homes.

The following morning everyone got up earlier than usual, just to witness the machines start and embark on working on the bounteous wheat fields.

Jethro Kiperng'eng and his two elder sons Noah and Faruk were there in full swing together with Kipwarir, ready to supervise the entire activity. My Grandpa, who was always a staunch supporter on such occasions, was not left behind either; he got up even earlier than Papa, took his breakfast and headed straight towards the field, his staff held behind his back with both hands, which was his usual way of walking. He was in charge of watching out for any looting of sacks dropped by the combine harvesters before collection. He was put in charge of security since he had served in the colonial army and he was very sharp and zealous with any monkey-business going on. Papa was in charge of arranging for the sacks of wheat to be properly computed, and notifying the co-operative society for transportation when everything was ready.

By midday, there was a small hill of sacks packed with wheat beginning to grow in front of Kipwarir's wooden house. As the days went by, the hill of sacks continued to wax as the wheat field on the other hand continued to wane. That whole week, the entire farm was a bee-hive of activity. Everyone was as busy as ants from very early in the morning till late in the evening,

The air was filled with the bustling and roaring of machines as they hustled ceaselessly throughout the day. We children on the other hand were not left behind either. We were busy running after the combine harvesters, hunting for quails, at another time clinging on the backs of the combine harvesters at work. Others who were slightly older rode on the tractors that were busy collecting the sacks dropped by the combine harvesters down their slides as they went along, to add to the growing hill at the farm quarters.

When we were tired, we would sit aside and watch the machines with great fascination and amusement as they dined on the standing wheat, munching and swallowing it, at the same time ceaselessly excreting the chuff from their behinds along their trails while internally retaining the grains.

'The one who designed this machine must have had a shape of a grasshopper in mind,' I heard someone put it. It was Kipronyei, the best humour monger. As my colleagues laughed at his comment, my mind dived into a shallow pool of thought about the idea in the utterance. As I scrutinized the machines, they were surely shaped like grasshoppers – bigger fronts and narrowing behinds, that is. Even the way they munched the wheat was in much the same way as the grasshoppers did. The only difference between them was that the former ingest and defecate simultaneously.

The harvesting process seemed to have gone very fast, something which was contrary to our wish. The end of wheat harvesting to us meant the end of an immense and jovial time. We prayed hard for the harvesting period to lengthen, a type of children's prayer that always goes unanswered. It was like praying for twilight to be postponed, which always happened to fall on the deaf ears of God.

Two days later, the wheat fields got their own back on the metallic monsters when the last kicks of a tractor rear wheel plunged it into an ant-bear hole. After the tractor was dragged out of the hole by its mate, the combine harvesters wound up their work, packed and decamped to another place, after receiving their dues, leaving behind them a hill of sacks which had grown almost to a mountain. According to my personal estimation, the mountain was built up of thousands of sacks; which was stupendous compared to the past years – a sign of a job perfectly well done and fat wallets in return.

When the wheat was perfectly weighed and packed into ninety-kilogram sisal sacks, Papa mounted his bicycle and cycled hastily to the co-operative society headquarters at Naseru Shopping Centre to notify the co-operative's transport department. The co-operative's ten-wheeled white lorry arrived without delay, to ferry the wheat. The lorry came for so many trips that I lost count. By the next two days, the hill had vanished. Everybody who had participated gave a heavy but a transient sigh of relief, for the first lap had drawn to a close.

Chapter Three

It was after a brief break that people disengaged their minds from wheat and turned to maize harvesting, which was by now bone-drying in the stooks in the fields. Funnily enough, most of the people seemed to despise it compared with the wheat. I bet that was because maize was only grown on a small scale, for subsistence, so using machines was out of question as it was uneconomical. Because of this the entire activity involved the use of family labour, which comprised mainly mothers and their children.

To us children, maize harvesting was one of the occasions that we embraced with mixed feelings, but nevertheless with enthusiasm. In one way or another we cherished it in that it was somehow beneficial to us. I am saying this because for every newly harvested maize field, we would flood into it with sacks to gather the gleanings, remnants of the harvests. I can recall that the best child would gather up to three or four sacks of maize from the already harvested fields, especially from the large maize farms outside our farm, which were harvested by machines. From the sale of these gleanings, we would be able to buy clothing and spend the remainder on year-end festivities, particularly Christmas.

The majority of the men by this time would not be around. Having received 'the share of the slaughter', some had vanished into Nondoreet - the district capital - while others, the likes of the headman Mr. Kipwarir, commuted to Loilrobi, the country's capital, on the pretext that they were busy attending to the matters of the farm in the offices of the Commissioner of Lands.

I know that one might be somewhat bemused and dumbfounded about where on earth the phrase, 'the share of the slaughter', came from. Well, I will let you know. I am saying this because during those times, there was a common but somehow primitive and outmoded belief that when an animal was slaughtered for a communal occasion, those who had participated in the slaughter must at least get a rib of the carcass each, even if the slaughter was meant for the common good. So some of the men, having received their fat allowances for participating in the wheat harvesting, deserted their families and left to go into the towns; with feigned commitments for their fat wallets. Some were even said to be attending bogus business affairs, weddings and circumcision ceremonies of imaginary relatives living in faraway places.

This situation was not experienced on our farm alone, but also outside. All the men in the region were on their 'cloud nine', bubbling over with transient joy and disappearing into the towns for fortnights, like Kiperng'ng, the assistant headman. Every so often I had overheard from the older teenagers, past the initiation passages, engaging in obscene conversation. Among them were Faruk and Noah, the sons of Jethro Kiperg'eng, who were two of the more grown-up boys among the farm children.

What I overheard was exceedingly pathetic rather than amusing. They had said that during such high seasons, all the regional towns, including Nondoreet, our district capital, swarmed with women prostitutes, who I later on in life learnt to be commercial sex workers. All the prostitutes towards the end of the year migrated from other towns in the country, even as far as from the coastal regions, to supply the higher demand of this region, assisting the ignorant men by budgeting for them on how to spend their hard-earned money, for which they had toiled throughout the year.

'Women, especially prostitutes, my friends,' Faruk, the assistant headman's elder son was saying, 'are devils. You keep them with a full purse in the morning but by the end of the day they will have drained it all, leaving you dead broke. If you are not careful, you will come home wearing only a raincoat which acts as a shirt, trousers and a coat, as well as their underpants.' He uttered his final words laughing hysterically. There was a kind of a story in public domain doing rounds that his father Jethro Kiperg'eng had at one time fell prey of the same, coming home with only a raincoat, but that was a long time ago, before we were even born.

As the men enjoyed themselves thoughtlessly in the clubs and bars, tanking up and drowning themselves in drink, some falling into the clutches of the so-called harlots, we at home were busy harvesting the corn, gathering the gleanings and pocketing the coins. Once too often at this time, we would get wind that Jackton Kipwarir and his colleagues, who were thought to be attending to the matters of the farm in Loilrobi, Kalyaland's main capital, had been seen moving about, beating their chests, with their heads high in the air bragging and shouting their ignorance from the rooftops, even in front of the greedy top dogs holding high positions in Mr. Elder Statesman's government.

'Kipwarir is taking a great risk,' I once heard Papa saying to Mama one evening while we were taking our twilight meals. 'Imagine - right now he is boasting in the city before every top official about the progress of the farm which he claims to own. That is like spilling the millet before starving fowls or displaying mouth-watering chunks of meat before a greedy hyena. Furthermore, you do not advertise your ignorance, because the elite will cash in and make capital out of it.' He spoke with a lot of concern.

'These deals about getting the title deeds of this land need to be done in secret, or else the men of greed and dishonour, men who do not sleep, will come to grab it. I am worried,' he said thoughtfully.

'Father of the young ones, you are quite enlightened and you are the one that should help the headman understand the cost of his ignorance, because this is going to cost a lot to everybody,' Mama had said meditatively.

'When an old man, who you expect to rely on, loses his sense of direction, who else do you expect to gain it?' Grandpa chipped in.

'On top of that, how do you expect such a bigheaded, headstrong and uneducated man to accept a piece of advice from someone who is twenty years his junior?' Papa defended himself, thinking hard. 'Trying to advise him is like trying to teach an old woman on how to suck eggs,' he added

'But if a fool can sometimes give a counsel to a wise man, how can such an elderly man not accept an advice from younger brains?' Mama uttered.

'You understand how crusty, peevish, snobbish and rigid he is,' Papa defended himself further.

'Any way, pride comes before a fall. I see smoke, and the fire might soon follow,' Mama said, rising up to take my younger sister Tatamei to bed, who was by then fast asleep on Mama's lap. Papa let out a heavy sigh as everyone retired to bed.

That night I stayed awake late as I tried to delve into the deep reservoir of my parent's untold concern. I did not find any reason, so in retrospect I worked out that I was but small-brained. But it occurred to me that there is always a lot to fear when there is a lot to lose. As I went further afield, puzzling about the genesis of my parent's worries, it occurred to me that the farm members had not acquired full ownership of the farmland, but were only squatting on it. Many a time in such sensitive issues, one was not supposed by any means to tell tales outside of the farm. In one way or another, we were all living in a glass house and were by all means not supposed to throw stones haphazardly, as the headman was busy doing, lest we break the glass and attract the attention of passersby. As for me, I felt that what was burning the headman was the false sensation of a fat wallet, since it is only a full purse that makes the mouths of men bubble incoherently.

Later that night, as I pursued the issue on my own, the headman's habit of parroting his concerns around the town engendered a thought in my mind of a fable about a certain noisy hornbill; that was by then common among the school children. The hornbill had at one time started making ceaseless noises in the forest, complaining about untold pains that were racking its body. Despite its endless noise, none of the animals had bothered to warn it about the dangers of his noisemaking. They condoned it, letting it go on un-cautioned, saying that the hornbill's noise was the hornbill's palaver, oblivious of the danger the noise was bringing on them. The noise in the long run ended up luring a hunter on his hunting expedition who came and killed them all, one at a time, beginning with the hornbill itself. With this afterthought lingering in my mind, a strange frightening spasm shot through my spine. I shuddered a bit and turned over to sleep.

Each festivity that year came to pass as expected, starting with Kalyaland's Independence Celebrations Day, followed by Yuletide which was one of our

Chapter Three

most awaited occasions. During the Republic of Kalyaland Independence Celebration Day, a great day in our country's history, which we were told was the exact day the freedom fighters managed to grab the wheel of leadership from their colonial masters, we would gatecrash into the few houses in the neighbourhood that used to own television sets, just to witness the big man, His Excellency Mr. Elder Statesman, presiding over the entire celebrations. This programme was broadcast live from a big stadium in Loilrobi, Kalyaland's capital, commonly known as the City in the Sun.

The most captivating and thrilling moment was watching His Excellency Mr. Elder Statesman, the sole head of republic of Kalyaland, inspecting the guard of honour mounted by the armed forces. We would hang on every part of his movements as he marched abreast with the parade commander, his aide and the Chief of the General Staff, his double-breasted coat flapping behind him along with the rhythm of the military brass band.

The other jolly scene was the march past which was conducted past the dais on which Mr. Elder Statesman would by then be standing in position, his chest swelling out to receive the compliments from his forces, a mighty show of proof that he was the one in charge. The march past by then would have been joined by other internal security forces, among them the General Duty Police and the dreaded Admin Cops, famously known during the colonial era as the Native Police, with boy scouts and girl guides bringing up the rear. This was then followed by another extremely buoyant and amazing performance. This was the fly-past conducted by the impressive and exhibitionistic air force pilots in which a fleet of fighter planes would swirl, ascend and nose-dive above the stadium.

At this moment, more often than not, you would hear trumpeting out from a radio loudspeaker one of the few television and radio commentators showering sycophantic torrents of praises upon the pilots.

'My dear listeners and viewers, my dear listeners and viewers,' he would say repeatedly in hysterical tones. 'Believe it or not, believe it or not. These jet fighters are flown by our own country's beloved sons, born, brought up and trained in our own motherland. They are now displaying their war skills and tactics to our father of the nation and all of us, a full proof that our sky is secure and safe from any foreign attack.' He would scream this out, as one of the frequently aired patriotic songs rallying people to protect their nation played in the background.

When it came to such utterances, I normally tried my best to maintain an even keel by examining such unnecessary flattery. Delving into the issue, I found that there was no jot or tittle of truth in the commentator's utterance but just a mouthful of sycophancy. There was nothing at all to brag about inasmuch as our so-called beloved sons piloting the warplanes were doing nothing but just advertising and promoting the products of first world countries across the expanse of our skies. Those whose sons invented the planes were the right ones to brag and not us at all.

Chapter Three

After these, the most eagerly awaited occasion, Yuletide, which was looked forward to with great expectation, was slowly drawing on as the days went by. People got prepared by shopping in advance. At this time, hordes of humanity flooded the markets during the market days, shopping around for Christmas treats and delicacies. All the masses working in the urban centres, including Loirobi, Kalyaland's capital, had travelled upcountry to join their families and kinsmen. Also those living with their families in the cities came back to the countryside to celebrate Christmas together with their extended families and friends. There were children visiting their parents, and grandchildren calling on their grandparents.

Every man who had checked out of the farm to the towns checked in again with a variety of shopping for their families except Kiperng'eng, the assistant headman, who was said to be still hooked up at Chepkinoyo, an estate on the outskirt of the district's capital, boozing up and perhaps attending to his reputedly toothless concubine. Kipwarir by then had stopped his noise-making in the city, arriving two days before Christmas. He arrived with heavy and sophisticated shopping for his family, ranging from foodstuffs and clothing to footwear. On top of this bulging shopping, he came with his usual questionable report, which he apparently brought whenever he checked in from the capital. All of it was just mere propaganda about the ongoing process of what was termed formalization for full acquisition of the land.

'You do not need to wet your pants about the issue anymore,' he would say with an ignorant impudent grin. 'Things are working well and the title deeds are on their way at this moment as I speak,' he would add with a lopsided smile.

All these words were directed at the other farm members, mostly men, who at that moment would have swarmed into the headman's house, laden with curiosity. Each one would be trying to keep abreast of all the matters pertaining to the destiny of the farm, as well as keeping up with the news about the latest happenings and developments in the main capital, without giving a thought to the fact that Kipwarir was in some way toying with their minds.

As the big eagerly awaited day hit the calendar, our hearts raced with overwhelming anticipation. Immediately the eastern horizons bleached to usher in the much-awaited day, we arose earlier than usual, at the crack of dawn, to prepare ourselves to embrace our long awaited day of great festivity before its sun shaded the landscape. The first thing that we elected to do was to bath ourselves in the open-air bathrooms around the farm's main borehole. Then before taking a big breakfast which included buttered loaves, pastries, cakes, milk shakes and several cups of milky tea, we would let the cattle, goats and sheep out of their enclosures, and direct them into the fields which by now were open and free from crops, to rove on their own.

After this, we would go back to our homes and dress ourselves in our Christmas best clothes, which

Chapter Three

mostly comprised an elastic-waisted pair of shorts with neither noticeable backs nor fronts, and identical shirts. Coming to footwear, we kept up with the latest fashion, which was plastic shoes of varying elegant colours, smeared with milking jelly which gave them a glittery appearance under the sun's strong glare.

When we were presentably neat in our impeccable Yuletide best, we would march in groups with the girls in their elegant floral butterfly dresses, heading towards a nearby church, each one bubbling over with merriment. We were all heading to have what was always referred to as spiritual nourishment.

At the church we would have a whale of a good time, which included singing and dancing to Christmas madrigal chorals and hymns about the son of God born to a virgin, who later died at Calvary to steal the sins of the world away. These presentations were offered by different groups and families. Those who were from urban areas and city dwellers narrated their way of life in the cities, in which they testified that it was as a result of the grace of the Son of God, who we all knew was born to die for our unnumbered sins, was the main reason they were still breathing. Some went the extra mile of showing off their urbanized families, saying that it was through God's blessings and care that they were where they were. This could once in a while make some of us turn green with envy, cursing God for not letting us be born into such families.

After watching various Christmas themed concerts staged by jolly Sunday school children, we would break off to stuff our bellies with unbuttered loaves of bread with orange squash. On top of this, the elderly, especially from better off families driving in sleek cars would fish out a variety of presents from their pockets, ranging from sweets to biscuits and popcorn, scattering them all over the place. Like starving fowls we would scramble and skirmish for them to gather as much as possible, once in a while ogling their children who were adorned with expensive clothing.

Soon when the celebrations were declared over, we would leave at our own pleasure, heading back to our various homes. Sometimes we would head directly to the grazing fields where we would round up the livestock in readiness to take them back home. If it happened to be earlier, we would run in frolic after inflated balloons cheering merrily, others indulging in juvenile games, everyone's belly stuffed to their expectations.

In general, there was joy in every heart, glee in every face and laughter in every moment. For sure at the moment, the roads of our lives were like endless straight lines devoid of any bends, for we saw no ray of misery looming on our childhood horizons.

Chapter Four

Slightly older, when I was old enough to start schooling and had graduated to herd the cattle by my own, the moment I had begun to realise my fears and joys, strange things which multiplied my fears started to happen. In retrospect, I came to realize that it was the time in which the world was opening up before me.

First of them all, the school started to rob me of both my feelings and my time. Before then, the tales I had been hearing earlier from my two elder brothers, Kiptolo and Kilabat who were already schooling, the word 'teacher' in my psyche brought horrors to me of a person who was paid by the government to beat up pupils, forcing them to sing the songs of the aliens which had been inherited from our colonial masters. This notion had instilled untold fear into my heart but due to my parents' pressure and determination, I was compelled to put it in my pipe and smoke it. In time I came to hug it with open arms like many others as I dug out pleasant things that one could acquire through schooling.

Leaving the schooling alone, there were also some things that to me sounded like knotty, unsolved and complicated riddles taking place in the political scene. As the time ticked away, it came to my realization that it was also the time in which lust for power and material wealth was taking its toll among the current government institutions and top dogs in the country. On the other hand, politics seemed to be changing its meaning to 'an ego-trip to public office for personal gain.'

At that time, there seemed to be a filthy stench of rotting leadership that was beginning to pervade Kalyaland's political biosphere. The pungency coming off the putrefying republic's top cream filled the air with an overpowering stench. It got too concentrated, cutting across the republic's bounds over the seas, finding its way gradually to the doors and windows of the International Monetary Fund and World Bank which was said to be located in Manhattan, a great isle beyond the seas. These so called universal monetary and donor bodies at once threatened to shut their doors and windows leading to the republic of Kalyaland if the smell were not perfumed immediately, for it was too unpleasant.

As the days ticked by, more anecdotes from the political scene kept on slamming into my awareness. The country seemed to have come into an instant wakefulness. Maddened horses, bearing flags calling for political emancipation through a multi-party system of government, started to gallop harum-scarum at ever increasing speed into the already muddied political arena. Furthermore, a great many groups of activists sprouted and cropped up from nowhere in various parts of the republic. Some were spiritual, mostly comprising Bishops, Sheikhs and human rights activists. All of them seemed to have been triggered by how Mr. Elder Statesman's government was engaging in oppressive activities. Some clerics were even heard shouting at Mr. Elder Statesman to ditch his staunch loyalty to a one party state and let people to decide for themselves and chart their own political course.

As these were still echoing in Mr. Elder Statesman's ears, rebellious political leaders had deserted from his government. It was said that they had differed with Mr. Elder Statesman's policies of government to join the religious leaders calling for reforms. But Mr. Elder Statesman, determined not to submit to their demands, had in turn answered them with an iron fist. He sacked and detained some of them without trial inside Kalyaland's most dreaded torture dungeons that I had once heard about, accused of thrusting fingers into the eyes of the father of the nation.

All this quickly appeared to have let off the steam of the masses. Both internal and external outcries at once poured into the country, each accompanied by fingers of accusation. All this was directed towards Mr. Elder Statesman. By all accounts, he was condemned for taking the country into rack and ruin by infringing so-called human rights and paralysing democracy. All these events had sounded like tales of the marines, or far-fetched stories, which to me were beyond my comprehension at that time.

Coincidentally, as the political cauldron was boiling over at the national level at an alarming rate, filling every heart with misgivings, there was a pot of administration gradually coming to boil within our home district - an event which seemed to have put the wind up each and every soul. The district's wheel of leadership was changing hands behind the curtains and new files were being filed at Nondoreet, the district capital. The amiable and polite District Administrator who had reigned and ruled the district with gentle hands was said to have been transferred under unclear circumstances. He was said to have been replaced by a brisk young District Administrator, with twisted and convoluted character that had succeeded in pushing him into prominence.

From what the masses seemed to have gathered from hearsay, there were dozens of reckless and shoddy allegations associated with his eminence. He was branded as one having the makings of a heartless tyrant. It was said that in all the places in which he had served as a District Administrator, he had left behind a trail of bruised hopes, bereaved hearts, agonizing cries and landlessness, for he had ruled with an iron hand. Moreover, he was well-known

Chapter Four

for using a free hand to attain his desire for material gain, especially when it came to land grabbing.

The news of all these occurrences seemed to have laden the air with an overwhelming pang of fear. This strange wave of fear swept through the spines of everyone, particularly those who were more vulnerable to the impact of the changes that were taking place at the time. Everyone in the farm started to live in great nervousness and foreboding, unnerved with horror of the so-called ruthless and heartless tyrant who had been cast by a quirk of fate into the district. To tell the truth, fright was instilled in everyone's heart, replacing in the twinkling of an eye, the buoyancy and blithe-heartedness which had beamed from every face and engulfed every heart.

In the midst of all this, field preparations were taking place, ploughing, tilling and harrowing the wheat and maize fields ready for planting. Noises of roaring, bellowing and wailing tractors of a variety of models filled the air, each seeming to be trying to display its strength in the ploughing contest. In addition to all these noises, the burning of dry wheat straw and maize stalks was taking place, their smoke infecting the air with an acrid smell. All this seemed to have given a fleeting break by lessening the tension which had reigned in the air. However, the tension intensified further after a few days when Kipwarir, the headman, rocked the boat one morning, leaving many in the farm alarmed.

'Some people are real chickens in their hearts and I am better off because I am not one of them,' he had howled at the top of his voice one morning while we were getting ready for school. 'How can you, full-grown men, cower before your fellow beings?' he had ignorantly bragged, walking downwards along the farm road with his usual sidelong contemptuous glance, holding his staff by its end.

'Yesterday at Chesarma Shopping Centre, I told the area chief to go and warn, as well as caution, the incoming District Administrator in advance against bringing his unpleasant manners with him into our land. I told him to his face to tell the so-called fully-grown man to keep his disgustingly filthy and stained hands off our land, or else he would encounter men who are each one and a half men more than him. Let him come and I will show him our spirit single-handedly.'

Everyone had oozed out of their houses, with unwashed faces and wearing only loincloths. Some were peeping through their doors, to witness the headman spew his fulminations into the peaceful and still morning air with extreme bafflement. Others stood with mouths agape, as if they could see better with their mouths open, for they could hardly believe what they were hearing. My Grandpa, who always gaped at such utterances, wasted no time. Having been already awake, he got out of his bed slowly, wrapping himself in his blanket, and peeped out of the door with perturbed disbelief, his mouth hanging open slightly at an angle of mild astonishment.

'Who is this disturbing the morning air with such empty sentiments? If it is Kipwarir, then the old man

Chapter Four

must be off his rocker,' Papa said, emerging from the bedroom buttoning his shirt.

'Who do you think he is? He is your so-called farm headman busy going around the bend.' Mama who was by then standing next to the kitchen, her thoughts and feelings paralysed, had answered Papa without turning an inch, her eyes following the headman.

'Dogs that indulge in frequent and careless barking can sometimes holler things they do not know, oblivious of the risks involved,' Grandpa put in, his eyes fixed on the vanishing figure of Kipwarir, which was receding into the thorny bushes ahead of farm's main borehole, winding his way along a meandering path leading to the fields, as if very much unaware of the scandal he had caused.

That very morning, schoolward bound, a thousand and one questions crisscrossed my mind, as I tried to address my childish brain to the meaning of all that scandal. Unlike other episodes, this was the first that left me none the wiser, for I hadn't the foggiest idea why the headman's behaviour had aroused everyone's attention. As I came to terms with all that, for the first time I found myself aligning with the headman's opinion, for I saw no reason why such things should be that scandalous. I saw nothing wrong at all with the Kipwarir sending a word of caution to the incoming District Administrator or D.A. as he was known at the time. I felt it served him right as far as his habits were concerned.

However, this matter as usual did not remain in my mind forever. It was after a while that I came to fathom why Kipwarir's utterances that morning had been so blood curding, especially to my parents. According to Mama, what the headman had done was like twisting the tail of a ferocious, confused, stranger lion in a new environment trying to acclimatize itself to the new situation. In such cases, the lion may turn ferocious and no-one around might live to tell the story.

After this, the days elapsed as usual; the ploughing season came to pass, followed by the planting season, which was usually accompanied by moderate cloudbursts which were perfect for such occasions. All these events took place with little input from us, as school took up the better part of our time - we were leaving for school very early in the morning and coming back late in the evening, with the exception of weekends. Despite the days taking flight, there remained a nip of worry in the air which I personally felt was an over-reaction. In the pit of my soul, this told me that something was amiss, and that sooner or later, things were not going to be as before. Everyone seemed to smell a distant whiff of looming misery in the atmosphere for everything became lacklustre and chilly, and everyone waited with bated breath for the fear of the unknown to unfold.

Chapter Five

Whoever said that something which is much talked about already exists, and if it doesn't, then it is in the pipeline, did not utter an empty sentiment, for the much chattered about event and its attendant pent-up fear came into being much sooner than expected. It was an event which, in its impact, dealt outright a terrible blow and distorted the joy and happiness of our lives.

This obnoxious thing struck during a mid-year weekend. As far as I can recall, this horrific event was the first shock which shook me to the core to the extent that even right now as I recall that very day, an inevitable spasm speeds down my spine, effecting a replay of that malicious scene. This often leads my mind to start racing with frightening images of that horrendous moment which had made it indelibly imprinted in my mind, bringing outright discomfort.

It all began during one simple Saturday in the month of June. The day had broken out like any other, with a nip of chilling and ear-biting cold in the air as the brilliant morning sun smiled its radiant rays across the expansive fields. The long early year rains had been good, the entire squatters' farm was cloaked in a mantle of lush green, with earth brown and affluent in fertility giving life force to the new buds and sapling. The now waist-high maize crops and tender wheat crops in the prolific alluvial fields too waved joyously, as they fluttered in the morning breeze.

I had stared at this breathtaking land of waving greens with high sense of admiration as I led the cattle to the grazing field situated at the easternmost part of the farm. As I shuffled my bare feet through the dew-wet grass, I indeed felt that the land was a local-biblical Canaan, not only flowing with honey and milk, but also pregnant with grains.

On arriving at the grazing fields, I rounded up the cattle by shouting to the leader of the herd to stop, which was an old big-horned cow in the herd named Tuimet that was ever blazing the trail. Tuimet obliged my command and I ran ahead of the herd. At once the whole herd ceased to walk and instantly settled their mouths on the dew-wet luxuriant pastures, perhaps to break their overnight fasting.

After making sure that they had all settled their minds on the pastures, all their mouths at work and directed away from the fields towards an open land, out of reach of the crops, I made up my mind to venture inside the wheat field to hunt for mushrooms and wild fruits among the scattered trees inside the field.

Chapter Five

I made my way straight into the wheat field, wetting my feet in the cold dew trapped on the tender leaves of the luxuriant wheat crops, leaving a trail of disturbed dew behind. After wandering aimlessly like an idiot heading to nowhere looking for nothing in particular, I found my way towards a wild tree which used to bear succulent brown and delicious stony fruits. The tree according to our own mouths research bore much bigger, sweet and juicy fruits than any other such tree in the entire farm.

As I advanced towards the tree, my eyes fixed on it, my heart throbbed with delight at the sight of it. It was heavy with fully ripened fruits which whetted my appetite beyond reason. I rushed towards it with the blithe heart of a starving desert traveller who has come across an oasis.

Without wasting a fraction of a second, I climbed up the tree with the agility of an extremely famished monkey, my eyes shining with excitement. While half way up, I had already started to salivate. The birds which were having their breakfast on the tree flew away chirping and yelling their curses. Without minding them, I took up my position on one of the topmost branches, picked four juicy fruits, stuffed them into my already watering mouth and munched to my satisfaction, my eyes darting from one branch to another.

On top of the tree as I enjoyed myself with nature's delicacies, I could catch a panoramic view of the entire vast farm. The crops had now started to glitter green, full of life and waving their leaves merrily. In the southern direction I could see the farm's quarters standing in a stately line. I swept my glance from the farm quarters to the west then slowly to the north. My eyes caught the figure of my aging Grandpa cruising along the edge of the field in his yellow hand-knitted sweater, his hands as usual holding his stuff behind him, making his morning foot patrol in the fields. Far ahead I could see large herds of cattle from the neighbouring farms moving along the great motorway heading to graze in the government-owned land, the herd boys trailing behind.

I turned my gaze back to the farm quarters, just in time to catch a glimpse of my fellow farm boys led by Kipronyei, each bringing animals from their respective families for grazing. They were all shouting, whistling merrily and singing funny, childish and obscene songs which were not allowed to be uttered in the presence of the elderly, especially our mothers. They abandoned the cattle next to ours and straightaway headed towards my tree, following the trail that I had left behind.

'I suppose the fool must be perched on one of these trees,' Kipsiya one of my best friends at the time shouted.

'Let's look for that idiot, he must be busy constipating himself,' Kipronyei added as they all started to race towards the tree. All this time, I kept still on the tree trying to camouflage myself with the leaves with the intention of frightening them.

Upon reaching the tree, they scrambled upwards, each one wanting to be the first. They jostled and elbowed one another like skirmishing baboons, captivated by the heavy presence of the fruits. At first it seemed that they had not noticed my presence, until they had climbed high up when I frightened them with a well-calculated shriek. All of us being acclimatized with such jokes reacted with pretence of being scared by shouting and laughing hysterically.

'You almost scared the shit out of me Kipsisei,' Kipsiya shouted, taking a position amid the branches.

'At least Kipsiya's fright is better off than mine. I think he scared my heart to my behinds,' Kipronyei added. We all burst out laughing.

After this, everyone joined me in feasting on nature's overflow, each one of us stuffing our mouths with the fruits and once in a while spraying the seeds out. We did this as we enjoyed the growing warmth of the morning sun.

After satisfying our appetites, we started swinging on the branches and hurling the fruits at one another, whistling and shouting elatedly in great gaiety like monkeys enjoying themselves after having their fill. This went on for a while until a tinge on the back of my neck prompted me to look at the east. Alas! What I saw was so incredible and shocking that it sent my heart leaping into my mouth, leaving me tongue-tied, my throat running dry as well.

I glanced back at my friends who were by then still singing, oblivious of my alarmed looks, then back again. I thought I was dreaming, only to be reassured by the intense shouting and cheering of my friends. Believe me, there was a fleet of vehicles - a jeep blazing the trail, a green lorry filled with the dreaded Admin Cops, trailed by two bulldozers, cutting across the fields, all heading towards the farm quarters. To ensure that I wasn't dreaming, I rubbed my eyes to see if it was just an illusion but it was as real as the gospel. This almost scared me out of my skin.

'Look!' I screamed at the top of my voice at my friends, pointing in the direction of the horrifying sight, in a voice laden with fascinated horror. Like a radio that has been switched off abruptly, their noises stopped at once and with gasps escaping their mouths, all my friends turned their heads in a double-quick action bringing their eyes to look where I was pointing.

We were all equally astounded and dumbfounded as if an electric current had been run through us, our mouths gaping in the same angle of horror and astonishment. We were startled for a goodish time, our eyes trailing the dreadful horror-striking sight of the foreboding convoy, fruits that were already in our mouths falling out one by one without our being aware of it.

By then, the wailing of the jeep's engine could be audible as it bumped its way across the bumpy field. The lorry which was laden with the cops, who were by now clearly discernible with their black berets and maroon cardigans with visible black bulky patches on their shoulders and elbows, bellowed its way, hot in pursuit. The bulldozers, which were bringing up

Chapter Five

the rear and slightly behind, simmered and strained agonizingly as they tried to match their speeds with those of the forerunners. At once, at this sight alone, I knew that the eviction exercise was now obvious and certain. The consciousness struck back to my brain and I felt there was a need to raise the alarm lest our mothers be caught unaware, since most of the men would have gone out by then.

'It is the attack! They are going to bring down our homes. Let's go and alert our parents,' I shrieked at my startled friends who responded quickly. Within the twinkling of an eye, we were all down the tree, others jumping down while half way. Kipronyei nearly landed on my back.

When we were all down and without waiting to be told what we were supposed to do, we fled like chicks fleeing away from an eagle towards the farm quarters. With a speed equivalent to that of fired bullets, we made a beeline for our homes with the aim of reaching the quarters before our malicious rivals.

Within a fraction of a second as it seemed to me, we were advancing towards our homes and at once as if switched on, we all found ourselves screaming frighteningly at the top of our voices.

'They have come!' One was saying. 'The police!' added another terrifying scream.

'The bulldozers!' put in someone in a frightening tone.

'The eviction at last!' I found myself shouting. By then, we were all out of breath and gasping for air, our hearts racing with horror.

All this commotion at once sent everyone scurrying out of their houses in horror while others who were outside were sprinting towards us, their faces tattooed with fear. Kipwarir and his assistant head Kiperng'ng, who happened to be the only men around at the moment, were the first to meet us. With frightening voice, Kipernge'ng stood in my way, trying to find out what was happening. I just gesticulated at my back without uttering a word and sidestepped him, heading towards my home.

By then, Mama, who like everyone else had been alerted by our screams, raced towards me with a cooking stick and a frying pan in her hands, fear written on her face.

'What is it my child? Where are the cattle?' she asked with solicitude in her voice, spreading her arms before me.

'Mama let's run away,' I found myself saying, ignoring her questions.

'What is it then?' she asked shaking my fear-stricken, trembling body.

'Mama, they are police who have filled a lorry and a jeep coming together with bulldozers, they are all heavily armed with guns and might well shoot at us. Let's run away,' I said as I started to cry.

Mama left me and ran ahead just in time to catch a glimpse of the convoy, which happened to be in sight, majestically approaching the farm quarters. She quickly turned and raced back and scooped my two baby sisters, Chebusho and Tatamei, in her arms and dropping the frying pan and cooking stick in the action. Then by gesturing to me to follow her, she sent a terrifying long wail in the air, as she headed towards the railway line, I in hot pursuit overtaking her swiftly.

The other women, including the wives of Kipwarir and Kiperng'ng joined in the wails too, racing to seek refuge at the raised railway line while others were taking to their heels to take cover at the railway station premises. As I ascended the pile of earth which supported the railway line at its summit, the wails, most of them feminine, had intensified, punctuated by shouts and a deep masculine howling wail coming from the wife of the old Arap Nyongio. With long steps, I quickly raced up the railway line ascent. Stopping between the rails, I turned back for the first time since we had started off at the fields.

What I saw was appalling; the jeep and the lorry had pulled over to empty their occupants. The Admin Cops poured into the farm quarters armed with rifles, whips and clubs. Within no time, the area was police-ridden beyond words. Everywhere was swarming with black men in thick boots, darting left and right with their shoulder and elbow patches, wielding their guns, raising the clubs and whips as they sprinted into action.

At that time Hell seemed to have let loose of its demons and poured them into the farm. Every soul was on the verge of panic as the police started their ordeal. Many things were happening at the same time amid all the cries and terrifying wails that no-one could follow in clear detail.

Suddenly, the sound of a fired gun rent the air near Kiperng'eng house, drowning the continuous wailings. All the shouts stopped at once and everyone embraced the earth, by lying flat on the ground to minimize the chances of being met by the fired bullet. Instead of lying on the ground, I dashed above my crouching mum holding my small sister tightly to her bosom and shielded myself against a concrete wall raised beside the railway line and peeped on its edge eager to see what was happening from where the shot erupted.

As I closely scrutinized it, I saw the figures of Kiperng'ng and Kipwarir sprinting out of the assistant headman's house each holding a sword in the right hand and bow and arrows on the other. They had swiftly made their way braving the cops who backed off their way then setting on after them, shouting and ordering them to surrender at once, but the two men disobeyed and raced towards a ditch by the railway side. Kiperng'eng was leading, followed by Kipwarir with a number of police officers hot in their pursuits, firing bullets in the air with the intention of scaring them into yielding.

The two men plunged into the ditch in time and with an agility which left me somehow admiring them, placed their arrows in their bows simultaneously and aimed at the police officers chasing them, and sent off two arrows that missed them by inches. The police officers quickly stopped, backing off in fright. With surprised looks, each one aimed his gun at the ditch and tactically fell back, fearing to be met with arrows.

Chapter Five

When this was happening, a lot was happening on the other side. The other cops had stormed into each and every house hurling out the household properties. As I looked at our house, I just saw the crockery and cutlery flying out of the kitchen door while furniture was rolling out of the sitting room followed by mattresses and clothing.

In no time, all the household belongings had been thrown out and piled outside every house in a higgledy-piggledy unsightly mess. By then, the wails had calmed down as people were keen to see what was going to follow – and this happened to be the most shocking.

After every house had been emptied of its occupants, the two bulldozers, which had been parked aside purring, sprung into work. Both made their moves furiously towards the assistant headman's house to embark on their unsavoury work under the command of a pot-bellied short black figure who happened to be a corporal and an officer in charge of demolition.

As the bulldozers were about to bulldoze down the two-grass thatched rounded houses belonging to Kipernge'ng's family, the commanding figure gestured to them to stop as if he had changed his mind against it, then rushed towards the houses, fishing something out of his pocket which happened to be a cigarette lighter. To the dismay of many, he went ahead and boldly set the houses ablaze - a thing that I personally found somehow shocking.

When the grass-thatched roofs had been razed to ashes, he ordered the bulldozers to bulldoze them down, a thing they did at once, sending the houses crashing. The bulldozers left them and headed to the next house that happened to be ours. Being both iron sheet roofed and walled houses, the bulldozers ran them down like a dose of salts, flattening them with ease, then headed to the next ones on the line.

The exercises being a walkover to these metallic monsters, all the houses were destroyed, lying flat on the ground within a twinkle of an eye, except the Kipwarir's wooden one which happened to be much stronger than the rest. This had forced the bulldozers to attack it from the opposite side, which left it falling apart in halves, the iron sheets of the roof flying in the air and falling behind the bulldozer.

After the monsters had cleared their single-forked arms of their assignment with the headman's house, they pulled up beside the mess they had caused, senselessly waiting for further instruction. From the way they were purring and wailing silently, one could tell that they were asking for more. They were like two lions licking their bloody mouths after having an appetizing meal that had only whetted their appetites.

From the position where I had crouched still with bated breath for more miseries to unfold, my eyes, fixed on the metallic monsters, caught a glimpse of the inscription along the sides of both bulldozers clearly discernible under the glare of the mid-morning sun. From the little reading knowledge I had recently imbibed at school, the block capital inscriptions along the midriffs of both the machines were bearing the words MINISTRY OF PUBLIC WORKS AND CONSTRUCTION. I tried to digest these readings and felt that there was a mistake done by the one who wrote those words because to me, it should have been erased and corrected to read MINISTRY OF PUBLIC MESS AND DESTRUCTION instead.

While this was crossing my mind, a certain bellowing voice calling for attention hit the ear. As I lifted my gaze, I found that it was coming from the stocky paunchy figure in charge of the exercise.

'Now my dear friends, the dwellers of these demolished dwellings,' he was saying, his nape almost exploding and his pot-like belly rising and falling with each and every word.

'Listen and get it right into your ears. We are working under an order of the new District Administrator who has discovered that you are squatting on this piece of land illegally. What we have carried out is nothing but a mere notification, not in the written form but by action. That is why we haven't laid our tactful hands on anyone or manhandled anybody,' he went on, heaving heavily.

'And for the two old men who call themselves the heads of this farm and who are right now busy hiding in the ditch thinking they can retaliate against us, I want to tell you that you are no match to us in anyway,' he said, pointing in a threatening way with his shiny swagger cane in the direction of where Kipwarir and Kipernge'ng were taking cover.

'I want you to know that we have not put you under arrest because you have outmatched us, but only because we have pitied you. Therefore you are required to quit the land as soon as possible, if you do not want to be caught by the next plague which will be more severe and adverse than this.' He completed his unpleasant impromptu speech and shouted to his men to board the lorry as he climbed into the front of the jeep.

With lightning speed, the police obediently scrambled up into the waiting lorry, and in no time they were being hurriedly ferried away in the same order as that in which they had come, with them in the middle and the bulldozers bringing up the rear. They left as if very much untouched by the wanton destruction of property and the sorry sight that was a result of the havoc they had senselessly committed and were now leaving behind. To cap it all, they never considered all the agony and the panic they had instilled into our innocent young hearts.

Chapter Six

After the monsters and the puppets of destruction had receded into the eastern horizon, heading triumphantly towards Nondoreet from where they were being manipulated, people resurfaced, emerging one by one out of their hideouts where they had taken their refuge. They drew in their breaths, mixed with gasps of horror and shock. Their ability to think and react, driven away by panic at the sight of their flattened homes, seemed to have bounced back into being.

Mama, just like any other person overcome with curiosity to see what had been left for them by the plague bearers, scurried towards the bulldozed homes that were by now in a mess of dilapidated ruins. My two baby sisters, who had clung dangling at my mother's back and front, also seemed equally horrified for they just stared around. Like two terrified mice, their smoldering childish eyes were darting in bewilderment as they grasped tightly their Mama's body.

I quickly shelled myself from the pod-vantage point where I had taken cover to witness everything and shot off after Mama towards the line of dereliction and embers, where there had been houses only in the morning. To me, it seemed to have been reduced into tumbled ruins within the batting of an eyelid.

I advanced towards the remnants dry-eyed and with cold feet. The scenery was just a dreadful eyesore. I stared with vacant eyes at the odious mess and it was extremely detestable and hateful. All the household property had been hurled here and there in a senseless manner. The bedding, furniture, crockery and cutlery were all intermingled in a horrid mess. The one-time buildings were no exception. The doors and the windows were totally disfigured past repair, the iron sheets crumpled beyond recall. Inside, within the rubble, was a crushed sack of maize, slashed and spilling the grains anyhow, which was an abominable and heavy sin.

A smouldering fire's acrid smoke coming off Kiperng'eng's burnt and tumbled house seared through the air, choking every nostril. The house had been razed to ashes and amid the debris rafters were charred to nothing. My two elder brothers, Kiptolo and Kilabat, and Kipwarir's older son Kibelat, who happened to have gone for an adventure walk in the neighbourhood, came running, breathing heavily, panting with eyes wide open in disbelief and astonishment as they tried to come to terms with the devastating sight. The homes which they had left that very morning safe and sound greeted them with emptiness in a state of destruction.

I had been so totally carried away by the appalling event that I was not aware of the railway line on the crest of the hill which had been filled chock-a-block by a multitude of onlookers, mostly the outsiders who had gathered to watch the live and heartless, obnoxious film unfold. Others were musing over the whole thing. Some maintained solemn looks, arms folded across their chests, while a few shook their heads in a moving way as they ambled away, one by one with bent postures and drooping shoulders.

In the midst of the aftershock, everyone started to get down to the business of trying tidying up the hideous mess of household properties which were strewn around. I helped my Mama to sort the intermingled household properties, as my brothers gathered and winnowed the spilled and soiled maize grains which had been crashed and sliced out their sacks by the bulldozers. My two baby sisters who by then had been lowered down by Mama were just seated there without uttering any of their usual infant babble, their eyes darting from one place to another.

Papa, who had left by bicycle at the crack of dawn for Nondoreet, the district capital, burst in on us cycling very hard, his legs moving up and down like pistons under acceleration. Arriving at the debris and annihilation of our home, he dismounted his boneshaker, breathing sharply in his anger. His eyes were blood-shot which indicated that he was very hot under the collar, fuming furiously inside. For a while, he stood breathless before the vandalized home, arms akimbo, and glared resentfully at the debris with abhorrence and detestation. From his appearance it seemed that he was trying to come to terms with the embittering sight and making sure he was not hallucinating.

It did not take me long to tell from his countenance the sort of a battle that was taking place in the pit of his soul. Being a sole breadwinner and the head of family, he was pondering how he was going to shelter and fend for his family of six which had been rendered homeless. Here were his six offspring; amongst them two baby daughters who were highly delicate and not fit to be exposed to sun, cold and rain. As it was a rainy season which harboured the breeding of mosquitoes, zillions of them were waiting to feast on our blood immediately darkness blanketed the land.

He then moved around the annihilation shaking his head in vehement protest as he examined the extent of the damage.

'You mean there was no man in the entire farmstead to stop all this from happening? This is supposed only to happen over the dead bodies of men,' he said, with clenched teeth biting his lower lip in anger. No-one answered. We all stared at him as he moved around the debris, seemingly lost in thought.

In all sincerity, my father was a man of few words, slow to anger but when infuriated he could get out of hand. This was well-known to everyone in the entire farmstead. Some had attributed this character by alluding that by virtue of our family's totem being a bee, his character resembled that of a bee in one way or another. He was an inoffensive bee when undisturbed but could turn wild when provoked. Furthermore, while speaking, he picked and chose his words quite carefully as though every word that came out of his mouth cost him a jingle of pennies.

Mama had warned us from time to time against doing anything that could upset him. We had not taken much notice of this until the time when he had beaten up my younger brother. This had made us realize that he was indeed the type that can beat the living daylights out of one. My brother had scooped a handful of soil and put it into the water troughs containing water that was used to water the cattle at the farm's main borehole. In return for this he had received a severe beating with the buckle of our father's leather belt.

By midday, the sea of humanity that had thronged and filled the crest of the railway line had vanished one by one like morning dew escaping the glare of the sun, perhaps to attend to their own business. There were only few passers-by; especially cyclists, who kept on throwing quick and sharp glances at the vandalized homes as they cycled along a narrow side-walk that went alongside the railway line.

Just then, some outsiders who were the closest friends and relatives of the various families in the farmstead, particularly those who happened to be living within the vicinity, poured in to commiserate with us over our predicament and to give us solace. From my personal analysis, the mouth of every visitor that called into the farm pronounced a store-full of curses and abominations, all angled to the ones who had carried out the exercise.

The first relative to call on us was my paternal cousin Truphosa, a daughter to my only aunt. She was married to a tin of salt- and a perpetual drunkard, the son of an ex-chief who owned a gigantic tract of land stretching from behind the railway for nearly a kilometre southwards. For some strange and startling reason, as it seemed to me, she flung herself into Mama'sarms, who by then had stopped whatever she was doing to welcome her. In a flurry of grief, she started to weep tremblingly like somebody mourning the death of a next of kin. This seemed to have brought the reality of the situation home to my mother, since she too broke into sobs. They both seemed equally emotional.

Everyone around stopped doing whatever they were doing and stared at the two grieving souls. I felt my heart strings tugged by the sight and tears stung my eyes as I admired such a concern that one could have for her uncle's family predicament, which they had been subjected to by what seemed like sadistic motives.

Meanwhile, Papa had recovered from the shock and he was once more back to himself. He had stopped soliloquizing and had got down to the business of trying to sort out the crippled iron sheets, which had partly survived the vandalism. On hearing the sobs, he just threw a quick glance at the grieving figures and went on with his business.

For a while, Mama and Truphosa held each other comfortingly before getting their composure back. She withdrew her embrace from Mama and walked past me to where papa was, patting my head with her right hand and her left wiping her tears with the corner of her wrapper.

Papa took a little while before turning bolt upright to his niece. He offered his hand to her, eyeing her depressed state.

'My sister's daughter, we have been struck by a plague at last,' Papa said hoarsely.

'Worry less uncle, the just and the righteous one who is above all the authorities is watching from above and I am doubly sure he too is not at all happy about it all,' she said sadly in a consoling tone.

'You are absolutely right my niece, I too believe that the most high must have looked down and shed a tear,' Papa agreed, gesturing heavenwards.

'Precisely uncle, the vengeance is his; on top of that all, he says that we must not fear the one who can destroy you physically but the one who can annihilate the spirit and soul,'she uttered meditatively, gazing at the debris.

Every so often when it came to such sentimental talk, I would try extremely hard to prick my ears so as to hang onto every word. When I had inclined my ears to catch more of their words, I was cut short by the bellow of a familiar voice coming not far from the farm's main borehole.

We all turned our attention towards the source of the voice. There was Grandpa herding all the farm cattle along a well-trodden cattle lane leading towards the farm's main borehole, winding its way along the thorny bushes. This borehole was where the entire farm's livestock were watered.

This sight brought me back to my senses. I had forgotten anything to do with the cattle. As it dawned on me that it was my duty to herd that day, I quickly came back to my own self. Since I was the type who hated being reminded of what I was supposed to do, I immediately abandoned what I was doing and took to my heels towards the borehole to help him with the cattle.

In zero time, other farm children who had immediately made after me had joined me. Among them were my friends Kipronyei and Kipsiya. We wordlessly watered the cattle in gloom. Some were drawing the water from the borehole to refill the troughs, while others regulated the cattle to drink the water in turns so as to avoid congestion around the water troughs which were made of half cut drums and old rear tyres of tractors.

The moment Grandpa had handed over the cattle to us, he wordlessly headed melancholically and in the extreme doldrums to the ghastly sight of the bulldozed abodes; both his hands as usual holding his walking stick behind his back. Judging from his gait, with drooping shoulders, he looked rather frail. He looked like someone out of his depth in walking.

Having done the watering, we sorted out the cattle and herded them into their respective enclosures, waiting to be milked.

After confining the cattle in our family's enclosure; which was just over the small road, I headed back to the destroyed homes. There, I found my cousin Truphosa back to herself. She had made a hearth outside, just beside where the kitchen used to be. She was bringing some water to the boil which was an indication that she was struggling to prepare the already belated lunch.

I personally felt no pang of hunger, however, and had no appetite at all. Grandpa was there, still somewhat tongue-tied, going around the dilapidated houses, striking the crumbled iron-sheeting with his walking stick and mumbling inaudible words which sounded like silent abominations.

I went and sat languidly under the shade of a castor oil plant which stood halfway between our demolished abode and that of our immediate neighbour, Tiebo Songhor. As I took a breather, I stared in melancholy fashion at all the flattened houses - such a senseless act. I found it unbelievable that human hearts could house such monstrosity.

The sun was beyond its hottest peak but its aftereffects could still be felt in the presence of a sweltering heat. The sky at that moment was clearly blue with no signs of rain that day, though there were indications that it was not further away than the following day. The entire land looked as if it were trembling with the sun's weakening flames, the district capital on the eastern horizon pulsating in the dwindling heat of the sun.

I shifted my gaze towards Kipwarir's domicile, and caught a glimpse of him patrolling around his bulldozed wooden home. From such a distance, you could tell that his blood was boiling in him, making him burn with fury.

Eventually we ate our belated lunch at around four o'clock, comprising compact cornmeal with milk which had been milked that afternoon. The milk that had been preserved in the morning for the lunch hour had been spilled by the bulldozers.

Meanwhile I took a keen look at everyone's face and each one was wreathed in gloom. Everyone wore a melancholic countenance as if they were mourning for the demise of the sun that was soon going to die in the west.

The twilight just like any other day drew in a minute at a time. It was quite clear that gloom would eventually descend upon the land. We had nowhere to live in and for that night it was certain that we were going to provide a palatable meal for the zillions of mosquitoes who by then I suppose could have been warming up, for that night we got a handful of bites.

At last, the day sluggishly drew to a close as the sun gradually capitulated its sovereignty to the darkness. The bloody afterglow suffused through the clouds garnishing the ghastly sight of vandalism with colours of blood.

Chapter Six

A cimmerian blanket of darkness fell upon the entire land and everywhere was dominated by gloom. As usual during the beginning of the night, everyone including birds and animals came back to their respective homes. The brooding hens cackled and chuckled around looking for somewhere to roost, since their homes too had not survived the wrath of the bulldozers.

The night was moonless and still, filled with solitude. There was no infant shouting as usual, or the howling of hounds. The night was extremely dull - heavy with quietude. We lit bonfires to warm ourselves as we waited for the evening meals that were being prepared by Mama on a different hearth next to where the kitchen stood before. Truphosa had left at dusk for her house to attend to her family. Seated around the fire were the six of us, my two elder brothers and youngest brother together with Papa and Grandpa. My two baby sisters were with Mama.

Every family was clustered together for some warmth as they conversed in low tones like ghosts in a nightmare. I stared at the faces lit by the sparkling fire and there was no ray of happiness in them. All my three brothers sat in a deadpan state, their heads on their knees and all of them in drowsy positions. Papa and Grandpa were both sitting on the stools, their chins cupped in their hands. Grandpa once in a while scratched his graying head in a slow motion with his wrinkled hands as if trying to recall something. His dim grey eyes blinkingly stared into the profound darkness as if trying to discern something hidden in it. Papa's eyes were transfixed by the crackling fire as if waiting for an answer.

Meanwhile, the supper was ready and we ate it slowly in silence like a tasteless meal meant only to fill the bellies and not to quell the appetite. After the evening meal, we fetched our bedding that comprised mainly skins and sisal sacks to lie on and the blankets to cover ourselves, ready to settle down.

We made our beds close together for safety and warmth. That night for the first time in our lives, we lay down in the open air. I lay down on my back and stared into the helpless heavens beyond the twinkling stars where God seemed to be hiding his face to avoid my myriad questions.

I remained in that position totally awake for a long while, staring heavenwards as a myriad questions crisscrossed my mind trying to puzzle the reason as to why God could allow such a man-made catastrophe to befall us. I bit my lower lip in bitterness towards all those who were behind the whole thing as hot tears suffused the sides of my face. I wished I was powerful enough to draw back the humanity which seemed to be walking out of human hearts.

Chapter Seven

The following day we woke up into a Sunday of a biting cold with uncountable lumps on our faces resulted from mosquito bites. The freezing blankets made our jaws chatter. I personally felt frozen to the marrow as I quaked, my small body doubled up under the blanket. Thereafter, we were compelled by the intense cold to get up earlier than usual. The cold was so unbearable that it made us decide to light a fire to warm ourselves as we waited eagerly for the sun to emerge, nursing the itchy lumps on our temples and our hands with mild scratches.

At long last, in the east of the ever-rising sun a half-veiled sun hatched out, giving an impression of a lopsided smile, upper lip recoiled in a scornful grimace as though jeering at the predicament which we were wallowing in. Consequently, it had little effect in dispelling the nip in the air.

After warming our bellies with breakfast which as usual consisted of hot milky tea, everyone got down to the tedious business of picking themselves up from the situation into which they had been recklessly shoved. The entire farm turned into a society of ants. The majority of the men went out very early to buy new building materials. Some women too left with sickles and ropes in their hands scattering into various places in the neighbourhood to gather the thatching grass.

We the children who had no duty to herd that day too had a bundle of work to carry out. Those who were too young to work were sent to herd so as to let the older ones do the work.

Many families opted to put up mud-walled houses with thatched roofs since they were the only readily available building materials which cost no money at all. These were what we referred to as the gifts and overflowing of nature. We busied ourselves the entire day with the tasks in hand. Each one seemed determined to put their distorted lives back into their previous state. We played a key role by fetching the water from the borehole and preparing mud.

Papa, who had left at the crack of dawn before breakfast to buy building materials in readiness to put up a new home, arrived back. He came in carrying corrugated iron-sheets and nails tied to the bicycle's carrier. My parents had opted to raise a mud-walled house with a sloping iron sheet roof to serve as the sitting room and bedroom. The kitchen was built with the crumpled iron-sheets for both the roof and the walls.

In the meantime, the news of the eviction had run from one farm to another as if the wind and the

Chapter Seven

drumming were propagating them. Consequently, more relatives and friends continued to throng into buoy us up amid our apathetic moments.

My maternal Grandma called on us that afternoon, accompanied by our younger uncle who was the youngest son in my mother's family. We ran with joy to welcome them as soon as they appeared walking along the road. Sincerely speaking we used to cherish every moment we shared with our maternal Grandma, something which had made me think that perhaps things could have been better if my paternal Grandma was still alive. It was said that she had passed away in the early nineteen fifties leaving Papa at a very tender age.

Grandma embraced us, calling out our names with a sorrowful voice. I knew that this was out of pity for what had befallen her daughter's offspring. She offered us fruits while my uncle produced packets of biscuits.

We led them into our half reconstructed abodes with brightened faces and a new glee on our hearts. Mama and Grandma hugged each other tightly for solace for quite a long time and by the time they withdrew I noticed Mama's eyes had turned moist.

'Weep not my children,' Grandma said consolingly. 'The highest official is watching everything from above; the current God is a young God who repays evil deeds here and there without a dither,' she added, heading to where Papa was fixing a door into the newly re-erected kitchen with the help of my elder brother Kiptolo.

She offered her hand to Papa who received it with a slight bow and turned back to Grandpa who was seated on a stool under the shade of a castor oil plant. Soon, the merriment of the arrival of our guests died down and they offered us a hand in the tasks we had been engaged upon, since we were up to our eyes in work.

By evening, the fruits of our day's elbow-grease came to something. Each and every family had raised their homes once more. The headman had erected a mud-walled house with gabled roofs, Kiperng'eng's two mud-walled square huts with thatched roofs which were the same as the other members' families except the family of the Old Arap Nyongio, who had put up a single large rounded hut with a conical-shaped thatched roof. The inside was partitioned into four rooms in a cross-sign.

Everyone called this day the longest day's hard work when the last red ball of the tired sun winked on our horizon. Everybody at last gave a slight sigh of relief since it was quite certain that we were going to escape the unpleasant mosquito bites and the freezing cold that night.

That evening, after taking a bath, all the farm's committee members (all the men in the farm) converged on Kipwarir's house to discuss the issue at hand. It was felt that there was an urgent need to address the problem by hitting the iron while still red-hot. At the meeting, apparently, all the members came to an agreement that farm representatives be sent that very night to the capital to attend to this pressing matter.

Chapter Seven

To that effect, Papa, who acted as the farm's secretary, the headman and his assistant boarded the midnight train at Naseru railway station, travelling to Loilrobi, the Kalyaland's capital to seek High Court intervention and file a suit against the government for what was said to be destruction of property, infringement of human rights and unlawful eviction. That night, after the departure of the farm heads, we slept soundly without stirring even a wink, in fact like newly appointed chiefs, perhaps to make up for the previous sleepless night.

The following morning, we got up earlier with aching joints and muscles, the result of being on the go almost round the clock the previous day. Being on a Monday, we prepared ourselves in readiness for school. We left our mothers and other family friends to give final touches to the newly re-erected abodes.

That day on our arrival at school, the farm children were eyed with curiosity by our fellow pupils. On top of all, we became the centre of attention in the entire school, treated like people who had returned to earth after tasting the sting of hell. Others were giving us piteous glances, others frowning at us especially those who came from the so-called better-off families.

It was quite clear that everyone within the vicinity had heard of what had befallen us, and there was no 'visitor in Jerusalem' at all. As a result, that day seemed longer than any other school day I had ever had before. We had a lot of difficult moments. Each and everyone of us was barraged with numerous irritating questions from our curious schoolmates wanting to know where we had spent the nights and if outside, how it felt to sleep in an open night. Many were curious to know how possible it is to spend the night outside with all those horror stories, which were drummed into the ears of many children, including vampires, the three-eyed ogre, night-runners and thieves.

For the likes of us who were calm and less talkative, it did not take long before we shunned these pestering idiots. To avoid any query, we pretended to be dumb and mute by never responding to their questions, but those with good natures, the likes of Kipronyei, listened to their pestering questions and ended up talking nineteen to the dozen.

My humorous friends Kipronyei and Kipsiya seized the opportunity to make their jocular statements and I overheard them during break time.

'There is nothing as pleasurable and congenial as spending a night outside,' Kipsiya was saying to a group of pupils who had gathered around them, curious to hear their grumbles.

'It is very great when you are bitten by handfuls of mosquitoes, you feel so nice when you scratch the itchy lumps, and in fact they feel so good, to the extent of scratching yourself continuously for two good hours,' Kipronyei added laughingly.

'What about the T-nines, didn't they eat you up?' somebody asked them amid the laughter. T-Nine was a short name for the neighbouring country's stray wild dogs, branded number nine, that were well known for transmitting rabies upon biting anyone or any other animal.

Chapter Seven

'Not at all,' Kipronyei shouted.

'T-nines are very faint-hearted and so simple to keep at bay. You just have to make sure that you snore loudly, baring all your teeth in a sneer as you sleep. By doing so, you are very sure of scaring the T-nines beyond Tangawea, their original home.'

I could not help myself being amused as they left their audience gasping for breath amidst the laughter as they raced to another corner of the field to crack another joke. I was somewhat impressed that even during a time of distress; some people can manage to create charm out of catastrophe.

It took Papa and the farm's heads almost a fortnight in the capital, attending to the matter. After twelve days, they checked in with more blood-congealing news, a thing contrary to our expectations. They said that they had succeeded in hiring a lawyer to argue on behalf of the farm, following the suit they had filed against the eviction. They said that from the look of the things, there was reason to worry. As they put it, there was a tough network of certain far-reaching forces operating behind the curtains.

It was quite chilling to hear that those who were at the bottom of everything, fighting to grab the land, were prominent people, millionaires if not billionaires. They were operating in conjunction with top officials serving in His Excellency Mr. Elder Statesman's government. The frightening rumour had it that those millionaires were injecting bribes into the judiciary and other machines of justice to ensure that all the farm's efforts to pursue justice were paralyzed. It was also another chilling reality to hear that the new District Administrator, Mr. Katwa Chelagat, was among those pulling the strings. To cap it all, it was said that they were even the ones who had arranged for the transfer of the tyrant into the district so as to use him as a tool to satisfy their materialistic greed. But then, I felt for my part that this was a fact that we had to swallow, however bitter it looked. We had no option but to put this into our pipes and smoke it.

My grandmother and uncle kept us company for two weeks before they checked out, back to our maternal home. While they were leaving, solitude crept back into my heart. That Saturday, I could not help myself shedding a tear as I bade them goodbye. I felt like clinging, imploring them to take me with them. I wanted to run away from the fear of the unknown that was biting my soul, but my love for my family kept me back. Each time I imagined abandoning them, I was afraid that something bad might befall them in my absence that would make me never see them again.

For that matter, we spent the remaining part of the year in great solicitude and extreme foreboding. My heartbeat paced with overwhelming apprehension at the dawn of every new day. As the days went by, a profound fear gripped my chest like a tightening iron band. A sixty four thousand dollar fear that kept on nagging and flickering in my heart was how severe and far reaching would the present malicious act going to impact on our lives; and praying that such fears would never materialize.

Chapter Seven

The harvesting season that year came sluggishly to pass; for we carried it out with zero pleasure, contrary to the yesteryears in which the harvest had been accompanied by great happiness and gaiety. The year-end festivities too were distinctly lackluster. We celebrated them in a deadpan and pensive mood devoid of the usual laughter and merriment. The common twinkle of happiness in everybody's eyes had abruptly vanished on that very day of eviction. It had been instead replaced with a frightening twinkle of fear.

However, despite this state of hopelessness and fear we had been plunged into by men of greed, we kept a stiff upper lip. I personally resorted to praying hard to God, who we had heard to be omniscient and omnipotent, to take us under his wings. We hopefully crossed our fingers and kept our chins up that the impartial God would come to our aid; but the hard fact is that man only proposes but it is God on high who disposes.

Chapter Eight

We marched into the New Year with timid strides, nervous looks, ears pricked and faces masked with fear. We were all alert and avid to see or notice any heralding sounds and sight of another imminent catastrophe.

We carried out that early year's activities half-heartedly, devoid of our usual enthusiasm. Although field preparation activities took their part in people's minds, it never drove the fear away. There was still that fear of the future which had been instilled into our hearts. Even though we hoped and prayed that such a nasty predicament might not come again, there remained a certain feeling that what had befallen us was just a portion. The wingless termite had come out to prepare the way for the real winged ones' attack.

Despite all these hang-ups and fears, we perfected the usual early year's activities as required. Land tilling was carried out in time ahead of the usual early year's rains. Planting season too was done as in years before, in the same acreages. Maize in March followed, and wheat which was sown in May.

However, when the days had gone by, tension slightly dying down, and the memories of the past incident starting to fade like legends in our minds, our fears were confirmed once more! Like the previous eviction, this too caught us off our guards.

It was almost a year since the last incident when this second one came. By then maize crops were some weeks to flowering and the wheat was beginning to be laden with grains. The morning was congenial, like any other, with bright sunshine. As it was a weekend there was no school. This meant that those of us who were not supposed to herd that day had plenty of time to while away.

When through with morning chores, we regrouped ourselves on the bare ground just ahead of the farm's main borehole, to decide on a game to pass the time with.

'Let's play hide and seek,' Kipsiya suggested.

'No, hide and seek is only interesting when there are girls around, right now we do not have any around,' humorous Kipronyei put in frowningly as the rest of us let out frenzied laughter.

'No, no, no, we can do without them, we are grown up boys and we do not want any skirt-wearers near us,' protested Kipsiya.

'I know you fear girls Kipsiya, you always get tongue-tied in their presence,' Kipronyei attacked him scornfully.

'I do not fear girls, the reason I do not want them around is that they are gossipers,' Kipsiya defended himself, feigning seriousness.

'Did I hear it right that you are not scared of girls yet you ran away from Chesambu when we left you alone with her inside the school's maize plantation?' Kipronyei barraged him further, his voice full of sarcasm.

'I didn't run away from her, but I ran away because I wanted to piss. On top of that Chesambu is not a girl to be associated with; she is so ugly, careless, and dirty. To cap it all, her mother is said to be a witch,' Kipsiya defended himself further, solemnly, amid sarcastic giggles and wide grins on our faces.

'Hey boys, enough of this foolish talk,' I cut in, in an attempt to bring the conversation to an end since I had seen such acrimonious arguments blossoming into fights.

'Let's play pebbles, I picked a lot of them yesterday on my way home from school,' Kiptesot, a younger brother to Kipronyei, said fishing the pebbles out of his shorts' pocket and spilling them on to the bare ground. We skirmished for pebbles like starving fowls scrambling for spilled maize grains. In no time, we had forgotten everything to do with the rivalry and in a frolic settled down to the game.

We had played for quite a goodish time, everyone deeply engrossed in the game, when repulsive familiar reverberations burst in on us. It brought all of us springing to our feet, gasps of horror escaping from our mouths, our hearts skipping a beat, ears pricking, eyes widening nervously. We faced the fields with stretched necks, anxious to find out the cause of the terrifying shouts, and just in time to catch sight of my elder brother, Kiptolo, the headman's eldest son Kibelat, Tiebo Songhor's last born Kimaru and other farm children who had gone to herd in the fields racing towards the farm's quarters at hair-rising speed, shouting and waving urgent signals and alerts.

At once we knew that the fears that had been lingering in our minds had been confirmed once again. Without batting an eyelid we took part in filling the air with siren sounds. Heart-throbbing shrills went out at once as we frantically fled in various directions towards our homes.

On the spur of the moment, the entire farm was in a pell-mell state as hearts raced with fire, thoughts going haywire. Like disturbed ants whose nest had been smashed outright, every soul was in mayhem. I personally was beside myself with panic; horror got the better of me as I re-lived the previous ordeal.

We had hardly crossed the road to our homes when the wailing of many racing engines came to our ears. Looking over my shoulder in a quick glance, I saw something which nearly froze the blood in my veins, all but making my strength fail me. There they were uncountable jeeps, many more than the previous ones, and a single lorry, all simmering and straining with the cops' excessive weights. All of them bumping along the bumpy field and aiming for the farm quarters.

This sight alone heightened my horrors further. My brother and his squad of sirens had vanished mysteriously into the thorny bushes, perhaps to evade the enemy who were almost catching up with them. I looked around the farm in a quick glance, and every living thing including dogs, hens and cats were already in flight.

The farm women, the likes of Mama and Kipwarir's wife, who were blessed with strong high-pitched voices, wasted no time in echoing our screams which at first seemed to have been mistaken for usual childish shouts. This alerted some of the men who happened to be in the immediate neighbourhood, who also acted very quickly.

With a speed which I do believe could have left the world athletic champions bewildered, I zoomed past our home, flying past Mama who was still moving about, hands on her head as she wailed in confusion, putting some fowls to flight, as I aimed for our usual refuge -the raised railway crest.

I was among the first to arrive there. I stood between the rails and turned back gasping for breath; my eyes darting in panic, as I tried to come to terms with the unbelievable scene.

At just a single glance, I saw something which almost ground my heart to a stand-still. About six jeeps, and a lorry laden with police officers, clearly discernible with their black berets and maroon

Chapter Eight

cardigans with bulky black patches, were closing in on the farm quarters in a high speed.

Hurtling farm men with flushed faces were rushing pell-mell, gathering their ancient weapons in an attempt to give their territory a belated fortification. I saw Kipwarir, Kiperng'eng, Papa, old Arap Nyongio and Andrea Kiperng'eng's brother gathering, armed with their outdated weapons; bows, arrows and swords. Screams, wails and shouts were increasing as the malicious jeeps drew in. Mama had gathered her wits back, scooped up her two panicking and startled daughters and was fleeing headlong to the raised railway screaming hysterically, once in a while turning back to look at the approaching horrifying fleet.

It did not take the farm men long to realize that it was folly of them to confront men armed to the teeth with sophisticated modern weapons, and outnumbering them almost ten times. One could not imagine how it would have been if the men had not turned tail out of it into the woods in the neighbourhood. Perhaps it would have resulted in a brutal bloody match of fifty wolves versus five sheep.

As it is said that the cowards live longer to fight for another day, the farm men took to their heels as the fleet of jeeps came to a halt and the cops alighted in a double quick action. I could see my Papa's black coat flapping behind him as Kipwarir tried his best to match his speed in leaps and bounds. Kiperng'eng and the other men on the other hand, were backing away towards the railway station premises. The old Arap

Nyongio limped behind, once in a while stopping and pointing the machete in his hand threateningly towards the alighting cops.

In the twinkling of an eye, the entire farm was crawling with the more of the vehicles' occupants than ever. Everywhere was dotted with figures in black berets and maroon cardigans, armed with whips and guns in their hands, ready to carry out their exercise.

With darting and panic-stricken eyes, crouched between the rails, I stared in horror and disbelief at the unfolding detestable miseries. The cops were darting about around the houses, like excited bounds in search, looking out for any occupant. My heart missed a beat as I caught sight of the ebony, stocky, ugly pot-bellied figure in the group, who I assumed to be the corporal in charge. There he was, standing tall, alive and kicking, shouting and doling out his odious orders to his men with his thunderous voice, his black, shining, perspiring forehead glistening with sweat.

At that moment, the anguished screams and wails continued to throng the air. Heart-rending and heart-tugging shrills were filling the better part of the air, almost to the brim, till there was no room for any other sound. There was no sight of any man in evidence; they had all vanished into hideouts -some in the railway station premises and others in the neighbouring woods, to dodge a risky fight and perhaps their apprehension by the authorities.

Among those taking part in over-filling the air with screams was my Mama, Kipwarir's wife, Magdalena, the farm's famous high pitched sirens,

Chapter Eight

amid other semi-audible wails of other farm women, the likes of Tapwago, old Arap Nyongio's wife.

Without batting an eyelid, the police embarked on their horrendous task of bringing down the farm's houses; a thing which escalated the wails further. Unlike the last time, they did not hurl out household properties. Having no bulldozers this time round they used the jeeps to pull down the iron sheet houses, before setting those with thatched roofs on fire.

Within no time, the entire farm was ablaze, the air full of crackling fire and scouring smoke. Those abodes with iron sheet roofs like ours and Kipwarir's were flattened by the use of mattocks, axes and machetes. All the iron sheets were hacked into pieces with axes until totally disfigured beyond recall.

As this was happening, farm women were turning mad in a mixture of fury and grief, fully expressed with sighs and tearful wails. All the women were wagging their heads and casting invisible curses towards the burning and crumbling houses. Once in a while, a woman could scoop a handful of earth, dash forward and cast it to the direction of devastation, wailing hysterically.

'Tell the District Administrator that he is not burning us,' one agonized voice would say. 'He is busy burning himself; he is conducting his own funeral including the ones of his descendants,' added another hoarse voice.

By then, I was still crouching in my previous position between the rails, eyes wide in disbelief as the cops conducted their hideous assignment.

'The new District Administrator has committed the unimaginable,' I heard someone say at my back.

'Yes, he has indeed felled and split the *sasurueet* tree in which he used to shelter,' a different hoarse voice added meditatively.

I turned back to look at the mutterers of the words only to discover that they emanated from one of the onlookers and bystanders, mostly outsiders who had gathered to watch the free horrific film unfold. The crest had been filled with a capacity crowd of spectators who had come together to feed their eyes on the disgusting sight.

I delved into a shallow pool of thought, to ponder over what I had heard from the onlookers, only to realize that the so-called District Administrator was brought up in the same district, fed on milk and food produced in our region, schooled at the same place. Now that he had become the district's administrator, he had turned ruthless by waging malicious war against his own people. He was indeed busy biting the very breast he had sucked from.

With heavy hearts, eyes welling with unshed tears, we watched helplessly as our property of unknown value and our homes went up in billowing smoke. The frenzied wails had by then died down, diminishing into sombre tones. My mother, who had wailed herself hoarse, was sobbing uncontrollably, shaking like a leaf, my two baby sisters trapped on her sides, clinging against her, stock still, their eyes darting in bewilderment.

I could not help shedding a tear. Choked by my mother's emotion, I felt an overwhelming anger coming up causing a painful lamp in my throat, as hot tears coursed down my cheeks. Murderous feelings rushed to my heart. For the first time in my life, I wished I had power to mow down all those who were behind the whole thing, including the police carrying out the exercise.

As I was still clenching my fists blinded with fury, I was startled by an outbreak of fresh screaming. I looked around with my tear-dimmed eyes only to see everyone including the thick crowd of onlookers which had lined the railway line scampering away in horror. With my heart pounding in my chest, I leapt to my feet to look for the cause of the commotion.

Believe me; I almost jumped out of my skin, when I saw some cops, at full pelt making towards where we were. Without waiting for any further revelation, I scampered away for my dear soul, scattering the railway gravel in the act, descending within a fraction of a second to the other side of the railway line. On accomplishing the descent, I took to my heels into the nearby woods, my heart in my mouth.

Without looking back, I made my way swiftly through the woods in top gear, which I imagined had left many crawling insects, the likes of ants and grasshoppers, gaping upwards in bewilderment. I sped along nonstop as if a vampire was behind me, hot in pursuit, wagging its tail for my precious blood.

Suddenly as I was negotiating my course through a thick bush, I was abruptly seized by a strong arm in a mighty grasp that brought me to an instant standstill. I struggled desperately to free myself.

As I was about to let out a sharp squeal, I heard a familiar voice call my name. I looked up in disbelief only to realize that it was Papa. I let out a long sigh of relief. 'Why are you fleeing away; do you know that you can harm yourself?' he whispered, glaring at me with blood-shot eyes.

'Papa they are coming after us,' I answered in a quivering tone, my body quaking in fright. 'Which way?' he snapped anxiously.

'They are likely to be on their way into the woods,' I replied in an almost inaudible whisper, gasping for breath. On hearing this, he dragged me hastily deep into the thicket where we found Kipwarir and two of Kipernge'ng's sons, Faruk and Noah, lurking in the bush with eyes alert.

'Take your positions gents, they are likely to be groping into the woods; keep your eyes wide open, and do not spare any,' Papa announced to them in a low tone.

'And you stay back here, do not run any further, cops do not arrest or harm children,' he gestured at me warningly.

I stayed back, crouched behind a thorny shrub, and watched them disperse, crawling on all fours in various directions, sheathed swords dangling on their waists, bows and arrows in their hands. I fixed my eyes on them, fidgeting about nervously. Sharp in all my senses with myriad scaring images crisscrossing my mind, Any moment expecting to hear the sound of a gun or groans of death.

Strictly speaking I was scared beyond words and had developed unimaginable fear of any sight of the police. I could not agree with Papa's words that cops were harmless to kids. Though I was still young, I was on the ball about any goings-on in the outside world. Every so often, I had heard over the radio of some heart-breaking news, particularly from the Central African Republic which by then seemed to have been under a tyrannical rule. It was once said that the president had ordered the police to mow down school children with a machine gun. The children were said to have staged a demonstration to protest against the hiking of school uniform prices. The main worry nagging my mind was that if school children could be opened fire at in another country, what could prevent these cops from doing the same to us?

With this thought, I recoiled further and covered my eyes to avoid seeing any macabre scene, for I considered it less horrible to hear than to see any horrific scene live. Fiddling about with my fingers nervously, I for sometime remained crouching behind the shrub, ears pricked but eyes closed waiting for the worst. Then all of a sudden I thought I heard engines come to life; I opened my eyes wider as if it could help me hear much better. This was followed by the wailing of engines amid shouts of orders before dwindling away, an indication that they were going.

Stealthily, I leapt to my feet and crept my way anxiously with eyes wide, back to the railway line. Emerging from the woods I saw a thick crowd of onlookers that had regrouped, among them was my father standing at the top; staring towards our homes. Anxiously, I reassembled my tattered strength and ascended to join the startled masses just in time to catch a sight of fleeing jeeps, behind the smoky landscape, heading towards the fields.

'I wished you could have been deceived by your chicken brains to come into the woods. We could have slaughtered you to ribbons,' Faruk had shouted pointing his sword towards the receding police fleet.

On arriving at the edge of the maize and wheat fields, they embarked on a hideous activity which left everyone utterly speechless. The jeeps and the lorry slowed down as their occupants jumped down hurriedly, scattering in various directions, some into the crops, and others into the grazing field where the cattle were grazing. They were shouting in disorder like excited dogs on a keen search.

We watched in disbelief as they rounded up the cattle and stampeded them into the maize plantations and wheat fields, to trample down the crops. As if not enough they too raced the jeeps and the lorry along the fields, mercilessly flattening the crops against the ground in a heartless act. This sight alone seemed too painful for any tears and wails, for no-one even uttered a single word.

In perturbed shock and distress, we witnessed helplessly with hands on heads as the crops which we had toiled for went flat and dead. Amid the turmoil, I caught sight of my Grandpa struggling to control the cattle back, only the next minute to be roughed up by one of the cops. Later we came to realize that he had been handed several slaps before being forced to sit on fresh cow dung.

The horrendous, heart-rending exercise lasted for almost an hour before the entire farm crops were brought to the ground. After performing their monstrous task, the police boarded their vehicles and drove away as usual in a single file, victoriously perhaps, with a good report of excellent work done to the ruthless tyrant at the districts capital; without taking into account the charred debris and ghastly devastation they were leaving behind.

Chapter Nine

No sooner had the sadists gone out of sight than the people reassembled their tattered hearts and headed in slow motion towards the ring of embers with drooping shoulders as the outsiders walked away shaking their heads in absolute disbelief, others leaving with ominous gestures.

As the rest of the farm members shuffled their way back to the scores of tumbled houses, I sat down on a small hillock by the railway side, heart still racing fast while indescribable fatigue got the better of me. I could not believe that we were down and out once again, particularly when I recalled the mysterious, dreary night we had spent last time, associated with cold and hideous mosquito bites.

Struck dumb, with a heavy heart, I glanced far away into the flattened fields. In the distance, I caught sight of Grandpa struggling to get the cattle out of the crops, perhaps to save them from bloat. I shifted my glance back to the smoking and gruesome remnants of our one time homes and it were most embittering. I pursed my thin dry lips tight, a well of hot tears flooding my eye sockets, almost gushing into visibility. Deep in my heart, it seemed quite incredible to me that human hearts could house such unmentionable monstrosity.

Suddenly, I felt a strong emotion erupt up my throat, threatening to choke me. To stifle it, I shot up abruptly as though stung by a scorpion, descended hastily down the slope, zoomed past the gutted smoky ruins and raced along the winding path towards the fields, aiming to extend a hand to Grandpa who was still struggling with the farm cattle. I heard someone like my elder brother Kiptolo call my name but I did not bother to turn back.

I arrived at the fields panting heavily. The speed at which I had run threatened to draw all the breath out of me. For a while, I took a close look at the eyesore of great devastation. It was quite incredible to anyone with a sober mind to imagine that the ones who had mercilessly played havoc on the crops were human beings with human hearts.

After a slight hesitation, I hopped my way through the one-time maize field, which was by now down trodden and flattened, towards where Grandpa was wrestling with the cattle. I thoughtlessly uprooted one green maize stalk. Raising it up in the air, I charged towards the feasting herd of cattle that, upon seeing it, scampered out of the crops into the grazing field, calves capering with tails high up in the air.

When Grandpa noticed my presence, he shot a quick glance at me, followed by a long sigh of relief ending with a curse. Without delay, he fought his way out of the fallen maize stalks, mumbling inaudible curses. With the aid of his decrepit walking stick, which looked oily and shiny with age, he fought his way out, his dim eyes darting about like two blind mice. On getting out of the tumbled mess, he took a brief glance dolefully at the dolorous sight before wordlessly picking his way towards the farm quarters. He walked like a tired hound after a day's long tiring hunt, leaving me with the cattle behind. I trailed his receding figure with my eyes only to catch sight of a dry patch of cow dung on his behind, a true indication that he had been forced to sit on fresh cow-dung.

I withdrew my glance from the vanishing pathetic figure of my hobbling Grandpa and swept it melancholically across the trampled expansive fields. Now the once luxuriant crops were in a sordid state. I shifted my glance further afield and fixed it on the wheat fields ahead. There were some areas which had survived the destruction but other parts were over and done with, completely beyond redemption.

It came to my realization that the crops which had mostly suffered the brunt of the plague were the maize. It had suffered the main force of the whole malicious attack since they were more fragile. Unlike the wheat, their stalks were extremely vulnerable. To worsen the matter, the cattle had also cashed in on

Chapter Nine

this heaven-sent opportunity, making a hearty feast out of their predicament.

Alone, with the cattle, I looked up the sky blinkingly, rubbing the back of my neck and suppressing a yawn. The sky was serene and cloudless. Slightly southwards, towards the demolished charred debris, the smoke was billowing high in the bluish sky, slowly blowing itself into nothingness as though fearing to convey the acrimonious report to the heavens. Heating up, the sun too was beginning to send out its rays, making the smoky landscape seem to tremble in flame-like heat waves.

Unthinkingly, I stared briefly at the ruminating cattle before glancing back at the smoking homes as bitter tears stung my eye sockets once more. My small face tightened and untightened in agony. Two ibis flapped their wings towards the farm quarters, chirping sounds like 'It is too much, it is too much!' I looked up at them briefly and then back to the borehole, where I caught sight of the other farm boys, among them my elder brother Kiptolo, signaling me to drive the cattle for watering.

I rubbed my moist eyes with my palms as I started to move the cattle off. They responded positively as if they were waiting for it and started moving. I traipsed languidly, lagging a few metres behind the single file, my mind lost in thoughts. In the distance, I could still hear the dwindling cries of the ibis diminishing into the far west. Their faint wails seem to have changed the tune into something like 'They are heartless! They are inhuman! They are reckless fire-raisers!'

'Surely, they are the unparalleled curs and brutes of the century,' I seconded them thoughtfully.

At the borehole, I leaned against a small acacia tree which grew a few metres from where the watering troughs were, wistfully watching the cattle drain the troughs empty, as the farm's elder boys struggled to refill them. All was silent within except for the sounds of cattle hooves and buckets used to draw the water from the borehole as they knocked now and again against the sides; now and again punctuated by rumblings from the cattle's bulging bellies.

Still in my position I shifted my gaze haggardly to the farm quarters. The charred remains of the devastation trembled under the noonday sun blended with the sparkles from my home's crumpled iron sheets. I screwed up my face to see better; but the sordid sight was too upsetting. I brought my gaze back to the borehole. Every cattle's belly looked overstuffed, bulging sideways as they moved about lazily to shelter under the shady acacia trees that grew within.

When all the farm cattle had drunk their fill and lain down to ruminate, I pensively shuffled my way back to the line of no longer homely obliteration; leaving the other farm boys still dilly-dallying at the borehole. I dragged my feet, holding my hands at the back of my head in a stretched position, an act that my Grandpa abhorred because to him was like aping the bereaved.

My psyche was in a daze, stunned by the bestial act. I was much bemused as I tried to make head or tail of the probable reasons behind this unspeakable act. Now and again I felt like jumping high up in the air and crying out in anguish, up in arms, calling for the entire world to come and see for themselves this unsightly brutality of brutalities, but I took a grip of myself and kept my head.

I advanced towards our one-time blissful dwelling with tired eyes and timid strides. I rested my eyes on the trampled mess that inspired hatred. The smoke had faded away to nothingness, leaving behind acrid and scourged debris. Although it had escaped fire, our home couldn't escape the tragedy of devastation, however. The entire buildings had come a cropper. The iron sheets lay flat on the ground, some crumpled up, bearing innumerable holes, the result of puncturing with crude weapons such as mattocks, machetes and axes. Some were torn in half, making them utterly unusable.

Amid the debris were household goods; crockery and cutlery, smashed cooking pots all crumpled and intermingled in an offensive mess. All of them were useless. Furniture too had suffered the brunt of the tragedy. Chairs and tables piled up on one another, others with missing and broken legs. Everything piled up in a hideous manner.

Everyone around was in a daze, not knowing where to start. Unlike the previous plague, there was nothing which had survived the destruction. The corporal in charge of the operation seemed to have carried out his last threats to the letter. The burnt down houses contained nothing except the black remains of our one-time household properties.

Papa was moving about trying to determine the extent of destruction; or perhaps looking out for something to be salvaged, still burning with fury. Grandpa too was there inspecting the havoc with the aid of his decrepit walking stick, once in a while blurting out a curse. Mama on the other hand was standing aside, both her hands on her head, stock-still, her feelings paralyzed by the horrible sight. It seemed too painful for tears, for she did not shed any.

'The world must be on the brink of coming to doom,' I heard a husky voice put in. I shifted my gaze to the direction from which the voice emanated only to catch sight of my cousin Truphosa hurrying along with a woman living just behind the rails, who I later learnt was Kipwarir's sister in-law.

'It seems now days angels tasked with guarding of hell must be dozing off every now and then, leaving the hell gates ajar setting loose the demons that has been of late anyhow rushing into human hearts,' added the other woman, as they approached our empty homes.

'Do not joke my sister, today's God is much younger and more vigilant, he repays evil deeds here and there without hesitation,' Truphosa added as she parted from her companion, who diverged to the assistant headman's home, while she hastened to where we were. I was struck by her words because they were the very words that our Grandmother had uttered sometime back.

For the remaining part of that afternoon, we did nothing other than sit aside and watch the dilapidated homes with helpless glances as each and every soul tried to come to terms with the present shocking and unsightly wreckage. Even time took on a slow pace as if purposely to prolong the daylight to let the ugly sight taunt our psyches, which seemed to be pleading for vengeance. However, the twilight trickled in, a second at a time, which piled up into minutes and finally to hours. The dusk crept in gradually as if too afraid to cover up the results of the unspeakable bestial act. The birds of the air were hurrying eastwards to roost. Each seemed to be looking down and pitying us, who unlike them had nowhere to roost.

Eventually all the farm children were assembled together and ordered to light a bonfire next to the cattle enclosures so as to save us from the impending danger of freezing in the biting cold, as we waited for another tomorrow. As I lay on my back on the grass beside the fire amid the drowsy farm children, I felt weary and my body failed to respond to my will. I stared with half-opened eyes at the zillions of blood suckers who at that moment were buzzing around, warming up for yet another great feast later that night, before sleep sympathized with me and carried away my consciousness to the blissful world of slumberland.

Chapter Ten

The next morning at sunrise, after a hasty breakfast, an impromptu farm meeting was called. All the members of the farm regardless of age and gender - something which was unusual -gathered in an open place between the farm's borehole and the cattle byres adjacent to the spreading wattle trees.

We sat down anxiously amid our mothers, waiting for the heads and men who were by then seated on the raised ground in front of us, waiting for them to pronounce what they had for us.

When everyone had settled down, Kiperng'eng the deputy headman rose up in a sombre mood. He cleared his throat, which was the usual thing expected of a man before making an address. He looked around as if either counting those who were not paying attention or those who had absented themselves. Everyone seemed to have swallowed his or her smiles for each and every one maintained a solemn mood.

Chapter Ten

'Our beloved wives and children'. He broke the silence in an unusually low tone as he cleared his throat.

'We must admit that we tender unreserved apology for not having been able to protect you from all these predicaments. I think that according to the ways of our culture, a man is not a man if he is not capable of protecting his household and neighbourhood at large. The women nodded. 'For this reason we are now going to lay down strategies,'he went on. All was silent except for a cough and a sneeze now and again that punctuated his speech.

'We as men of this farm have felt that we cannot go on sitting back and watching our tormentors torment us without even raising a finger. Before we resort to violence, we will first make a peaceful attempt. We will all hire a bus and travel to the palace of the father-of-the nation in Nukuoro and try to see if we can get a chance to express our grievances. We know that it is very hard to get an audience, but it is said that before you give up, give a try. Moreover, you never know till you have tried.'

The mention alone about an attempt to meet His Excellency Mr. Elder Statesman in his palace of palaces raised the eyebrows of each and every one of us. To me, the mention of this great, important man filled my heart with awe. It was only two weeks ago that I had set my eyes on him live for the first time in my life. It had happened that pageantry morning in the middle of the first lesson at school when an unusual bell was rung. We had rushed out of curiosity to the assembly grounds trying to guess the probable reason behind such an unusual bell. When we had all stood still, our school's headmaster broke the news as we listened to him with enthralled attention.

'Mm! Morning my beloved children,' he greeted us as usual.

'We have heard over the radio just now that our beloved father of the nation will be touring the western part of our republic of Kalyaland on meet the people tour as well as to survey development projects. He will be having many stopovers to receive regards from *Wananchi*. I am glad to tell you that he will be stopping at the Maili Nane junction. Therefore, I would like all of you to run without looking back to the junction; he will be arriving in forty-five minutes from now. The lady teachers will be there to guide you and lead you in praise and national songs. You can now break off and make for the junction and bear in your minds that discipline is paramount. The school prefects headed by the head boy will be on the look-out. Anyone therefore who shows any sign of indiscipline will be reported and I will spunk him or her to death.' He ended his speech as we broke into a stampede towards the school gate. We were like excited hounds, racing nonstop, aiming for the junctions at the highway.

When we arrived at the said junction, we were greeted by a sea of humanity from all walks of life. Thick crowds lined the highway for almost a kilometre. Businesses had come to a standstill. Once in a while, you could hear the high-pitched voices of women ululating while others busy rehearsing songs of praise accompanied by some dancing moves.

We jostled our way into the crowd, led by our teachers, before we took our positions along the wide road too. Some teachers every now and again kept on shouting at one or two naughty pupils, urging them to make their way ahead.

It did not take very long before we saw a presidential police escort car with a bluish siren blaring along to clear the road for the so-called great man. In the distance, chauffeur-driven sleek cars and limousines came into sight, speeding along the already cleared roads.

Abruptly as if switched on at once, people let out chants of praises, as ululations too rent the air. Others were waving madly the slogans of the ruling and the only party, some shouting themselves hoarse as they tried to express their staunch loyalty to his Excellency Mr. Elder Statesman. Some were jostling, pushing and pulling, short ones craning their necks to catch a glimpse of the big man. The police too had a hard time trying to control the crowd as others fought to wave their miniature flags. I tell you, a stranger would have mistaken it for the biblical triumphant entry of Jesus into Jerusalem.

The sleek cars, on arriving, ground to a halt between the frenzied crowds as Mr. Elder Statesman emerged from the roof of the black limousine waving at the crowd with a big smile. He just made his usual brief speech that lacked substance and proper goals, revolving around some imaginary development projects, before digging into his coat pockets where he fished out new bank notes bearing his image. He distributed these unevenly to the men surrounding him before submerging into his car as they started to take off.

This memory in my mind cleared off as I saw the people break off from the farm's meeting after Kiperng'eng, the assistant headman, summed up his speech. He had stated that everyone was to prepare himself and his household for the trip the following day which was a Monday.

We spent the rest of that morning re-erecting shanties from some crumbled iron sheets which had not borne the brunt so much. We were determined to get at least somewhere to shelter as we waited for God to pronounce our destiny.

The following day, we were awakened in the wee hours of the morning, before even the first crow of the cock hit the land. We got up and prepared to board the bus- for the great trip to the palace of palaces had materialized. We the children were ordered to put on our school uniforms-perhaps for the purpose of winning the pity of Mr. Elder Statesman, I thought.

Soon we were all inside a forty seater bus - about fifty of us. Some people from the neighbourhood were hired to look after our few remaining possessions and livestock till we got back that evening.

We arrived at the statehouse outer gates at sunrise, where we were greeted with the sight of the harsh-looking faces of the presidential security guards clad in green uniform, tight broad belt, green-berets and armed with sophisticated rifles. On their hips were rectangular pouches which I assumed to be housing plenty of ammunition.

These men, four in number, wore unsmiling faces and they communicated mainly by the use of hand signals. The one who says he cannot shudder at such a sight must be a big liar, for everyone in the bus froze in fear.

They signaled the bus driver to halt sixty metres away from the gate before one advanced to ask what our business was. I looked around and noticed that everywhere was fenced with a double fence, which had some electric wires running along it, making it look totally impenetrable.

When they learnt about our intention of travelling to seek audience His Excellency Mr. Elder Statesman, they first thought that we were mad and they said that we were in the wrong place. 'Did His Excellency send for you to come? As far as I am concerned we haven't received any communication that he has been expecting some visitors.' He had keenly inquired. 'Sir, do not even talk of having any communication. Even if he was to meet these people I do not think that by virtue of their appearances they deserve to be any near to a state palace.' One of the guards had chipped in before they ordered the driver to turn back before they change their minds. The driver had hesitated a bit and they went mad with fury.

'Civilians can't just come here and give us a hell,' one said, turning to his colleagues.

'We are giving you two minutes to get out of here,' he blurted blazingly, pointing at the driver who seemed as afraid as us. The headman tried to alight to plead with them, not knowing that he was asking for trouble. He received an electric slap that made him stagger back into the bus, palpitating his cheek in disbelief as the rest of us gaped in fear. It was at this sight that the driver knew that they meant business.

'If we call for reinforcements, some of you will never live to tell the story,' the one who looked to be in charge pointed out blaringly. The heads saw the danger and they ordered the driver to drive back to the provincial headquarters in the centre of Nukuoro town, the provincial capital.

We all alighted there to allow the bus to go for a mechanical check-up as the farm heads conversed with some of the officials serving in the provincial head office. From what I heard later, the head of the province had promised to order the District Administrator in our district capital to stop the exercise at once.

With brittle or rather empty promises as it appeared to us, we boarded the bus back to our ruined homes, praying hard that what touches the heart of God may touch those of mighty men behind these events, and on whose discretion, it seemed, our future depended.

Chapter Eleven

Back at our unwelcoming homes, living on the brittle hopes given by the officials in Provincial Administrator's office, our parents busied themselves in restoring the order that had been heartlessly and so completely pulled to the ground. Their determination seemed to hearten them as they moved on to what they hoped would be a better outcome – as yet unseen.

In two days' time new buildings had been re-erected beside where the other ones had stood before. Most of them were grass-thatched. Bearing in mind that the men of greed were not yet asleep and had not attained their material desires, we felt that the storm was not yet over and that sooner or later they would come back to put us through a further ordeal.

For this event we started preparing ourselves to work out how to counter-attack them, just in case they were contemplating continuing their eviction exercise. It was at his time that my Grandpa's skills, which he had obtained while serving in the colonial army famously known in those days as the King's Own African Rifles, came in handy. He organized us into various groups ranging from look-outs to different sections armed with different weapons. Though we had no access to more sophisticated weapons, we elected to use those at hand for we were determined to fortify our land.

Men spent most of their time making more arrows and oiling the strings of their bows. Our mothers too took part in it. They plaited slings for us that were to be used to pelt our enemies away. More so, every evening after school, we would move about the woods, machetes in hands, fetching bundles of sticks which we used to make *kiplutonok*-double-pointed sticks. These we knew, if thrown at someone at close range, would make his survival uncertain. Also, under the cover of darkness, we moved to the railway line to gather stones into sacks and distributed them all over the fields so as to provide enough supply for our slings, just in case the need arose.

When all these things were done, we started to train in how to use those crude weapons effectively, especially aiming at the targets, by using slings as well as the double-pointed sticks, of which everyone had gathered bundles. My Grandpa briefed us on some tactics concerning how to advance, withdraw and take cover. Furthermore, he pointed out a clever way of camouflaging ourselves in the shrubs by covering ourselves with grass and branches.

Necessity being the mother of invention, we did not give up on inventing more ways of fighting. It was at this moment that a brainwave came to one of us who suggested that we use biological weapons. It was from this idea that we decided to look for plenty of gourds, and moved about looking for swarms of bees which at night we put into the gourds. To our delight, the bees cooperated by accepting them as their hives.

We gathered a number of them and placed them in various thorny shrubs which were easily accessible to us. We planted several of them until we were totally satisfied that we had enough to hurl at our rivals in case they came back, a possibility which made us curious and even eager to see them come and repeat their former maneuvers.

When all that had been done, we just took our time to sit and watch out. At certain times, we farm boys were assembled together and given lectures by our parents, especially the men. They told us that we were living amongst our enemies, whose wish was to see us evicted from the land. In that respect, we were given examples. One of them was Mr. Arap Kirgit, an ex-paramount chief whose son, a perpetual drunkard, was married to Truphosa, my paternal cousin. This ex-chief was a stocky black pot-bellied old man owning a large tract of land, which stretched just behind the rails. He was commonly seen in his favourite black trousers, shirt and navy-blue half-sweater cycling either to Chesarma shopping centre or along the railway line.

We were told that such men were informers of the District Administrator and that very soon, when he saw that we had re-erected our homes, he would take the information to the tyrant at the district capital, who in turn would order his men to come again and wipe them out. Others were the current chief, known as Mr. Babenyu who had his office in Chesarma shopping centre. The list was endless and we were informed that another enemy was one of the teachers who taught in our school. We felt that this information about this particular teacher, whom we had nick-named Mr. Mathematics, was probably the truth. He was always harsh to us, especially those of us who came from the farm. In most cases he used to call us all manner of names such as rascals and brutes. If ever we absented ourselves from school, even when he was very well aware of the reason, he would always make sure that he had caned us severely before letting us into the class.

We were further told that these people were our enemies and were on the farm's most wanted list. We were advised that if we happened to come across any of them in a place out of sight or within the farm, they ought to be taught a lesson, or even wiped out of existence. We took these words seriously and heeded them and prayed for one of them to make himself available. Funnily enough, as the days went by, our prayers were answered - which to me came as a surprise, in that it fully proved that Mr. Arap Kirgit, the ex-paramount chief, was indeed an enemy of the farm.

This happened one hot afternoon, about a week after the last incident. Normally, there were some times when I would sneak out, dodging my mates, and get into a big bush of castor oil plants which had grown along the small railway line leading to the north. Here I used to sit, play and talk to myself without anybody hearing me.

I had come into this favourite place of mine immediately after the midday meal. The sun was burning hot, and the air sweltering. The district capital's towering buildings that were visible on the eastern horizon seemed to shimmer in flames. I sat by myself as usual and started to play; talking to grasshoppers that hopped in the bushes till something urged me to peep through the numerous stems of the castor oil plants to the west.

It was at this time that I beheld the figure of Mr. Arap Kirgit- the former paramount chief - cycling carefully along a narrow path leading towards the railway line. He was clad in his favourite long-sleeved red shirt, navy blue half-sweater, black pair of trousers, black pair of shoes and white socks which flashed at intervals as he cycled.

I kept my eyes on him as he cycled in a slow motion. When he approached the railway line, he dismounted and cautiously pushed his bicycle up the small raised railway platform. On the summit of the ascent, he stood between the railway lines and stared at the re-erected farm abodes. I could sense his malevolent envious eyes devouring our homes.

I fixed my eyes on him, starting to get interested. It was at this time that he was also noticed by Faruk,

Kiperng'eng's eldest son, who did not delay in raising an alarm.

'There is something for us to exercise our muscles on this afternoon,' he shouted at the top of his voice, pointing at the ex-chief who by then was still rooted to the same spot oblivious of what was happening.

'There is an antelope for us to devour!' another voice joined in.

'A duiker to eat,' added another voice as everybody gathered slings and double pointed sticks.

In no time shouts of 'Antelope!' had filled the air as the majority of the farm boys charged towards the startled figure of the ex-chief. Without knowing that he was the target, the poor man started to look around in an attempt to trace the sight of the antelope which the boys were making after. I watched with a mixture of excitement and horror as the farm boys advanced towards him. When they were about a hundred metres away from him, somebody made a blunder by shouting his name which made him realize that he was the one being referred to as an antelope.

What followed after this is hard to put in a detailed way. The poor ex-chief in a flurry of terror and confusion about-turned his bicycle in undue haste and mounted it as it went down the railway line slope. Unfortunately he fell down headlong. On the ground, he did not waste a single second, but hastily got to his feet and once again picked up his bicycle in fright as sling-propelled rocks started to fly over his head, one getting him right on his bottom.

However, luckily for him, he remounted his bicycle and cycled away at double-quick speed along the path, his legs moving like pistons under full acceleration, the boys still in hot pursuit. At last, he came to a big hut which was along the path, belonging to Taprantich, an old woman who used to brew illicit liquor. He desperately dived into it, he and his bicycle crashing in on the drunkards who were boozing up -including my Grandpa.

The boys on noticing this gave up the pursuit and made their way back, laughing to tears as they recalled the comedy that later became the talk of the whole week. I had by this time emerged from my hideout and joined the other boys who seemed to think that I had been among them. For some strange reason I did not laugh but was in a pensive mood. Later that evening, Grandpa came with more comical news which made everyone laugh for a whole month. He had narrated how Mr. Arap Kirgit had plunged into the hut on top of his bicycle putting drunkards to flight, panting heavily. He added that out of fear, he had heavily emptied his bowels into his trousers and pissed himself, making the whole hut stink with human waste, a thing which ruined Taprantich's boozing business. The customers were said to have called off their drinking for they said that the stench of human waste bunged up inside Arap Kirgit's pants was too unbearable.

To be sincere, this was the last time we saw the figure of the ex-chief moving along the railway line or around the farm's land, until some years later when we had already left the farm quarters.

The repercussions of our act of fearlessly attempting to assault or rather to wipe the ex-chief out of existence did not take long to bring a kickback. The idiot seemed to have rushed to the tyrant in the district capital and reported on how he had had a close shave, a thing which made the District Administrator Mr. Chelagat send back his men earlier than we had expected. It seemed that he wanted to avenge his informer with a free hand, but unfortunately his men found us on guard and, for this time round, it seemed that it was our turn to teach them a lesson.

The following happened one Wednesday afternoon on our way from school for a lunch break. We were approaching our homes, hungry and tired of the monotonous morning class work, when we got a signal from our Grandpa that our rivals were on their way. At this signal coming through, our hunger all of a sudden disappeared, for we forgot anything to do with midday meals. Within a fraction of a minute, everybody had been alerted and each of us was on his toes speeding along to fortify our homes. I had raced after Kiptolo, my elder brother, who was making for a small bush beside our cattle enclosure where we had hidden our weapons of mass destruction. There we pocketed our slings in our school shorts and made for our covers which were slightly ahead of the farm quarters.

As usual our mothers, on seeing us hurrying away with our stone-age weapons, started to wail in a mixture of fear and confusion, dashing about in flurry of perplexity. All this to us was a morale booster, as we expressed our boyhood bravery and courage. Within a split second, each of our mates had taken cover in the bushy green shrubs to which everyone had been allocated before. Here, everybody had placed his gourd containing bees that we had been occasionally monitoring, just to ensure that they were always inhabited. Since we had scattered the small stones everywhere, we had no worry about supplies for our slings.

'Take your positions; make sure you cover yourselves from their view,' came the commanding voice of our invisible Grandpa who we later realized had holed himself up inside a shallow ant-bear hole.

With a mixture of fear and excitement, I took my position in the cover as my heart pounded like that of a sheep in a slaughter house. Normally, I was somewhat chicken-hearted by nature but it seemed that the usual heartless attacks on our homes by these ill-natured men had hardened me. It was at this moment that I even realized that there was no elderly able-bodied man within sight except Grandpa- our brilliant septuagenarian commander who was clearly shouting out orders and pointing out to us where to take quick cover, especially by the main routes that our rivals used to follow.

I breathlessly crouched inside a bushy green shrub where I had placed my biological grenade, with my eyes wide facing ahead, my hands shaking in fright. As I peered through the shrubs, there I beheld a lorry bumping towards us and as usual filled with the cops. On seeing this, my heart pumped faster, making my body quake, but I was still determined to carry out my mission. I stealthily groped for my sling in my pocket and held it in my hand, picking up two stones which I had earlier placed there. With all these in my left hand, I cautiously reached for the gourd which I had confirmed to be okay as bees were moving in and out in their usual beehive activity, quite unaware that the time for them to serve their intended purpose had finally materialized.

On fetching the gourd, I carefully uprooted a handful of grass and sealed its exit in order to infuriate the bees. I held the open end of the gourd ready to hurl at the target that was at the moment drawing in with a moderate speed. To our advantage and relief, there was only a single lorry that had come to carry out the eviction that day.

With rapt attention, I watched the lorry advance directly towards us, totally oblivious of the ambush which we had laid. As the lorry drew closer, tension intensified and I assumed that my mates were undergoing the same. On our backs, the wails and screams of our mothers were hotting up, bringing into our ears a provocative call for protection.

In the twinkling of an eye, the lorry was there before us zigzagging through the shrubs. With overwhelming mixture of bitterness and fury, I shook the gourd containing the bees vigorously until I heard them fuming and complaining in anger wanting to be let out to direct their pent-up anger onto whoever was troubling them. When the lorry was about twenty meters away, I hurled the gourd towards it. The gourd landed right inside the trailer where the police were. This was followed by numerous more from my colleagues.

What followed here is very hard for me to recount in an elaborate way, as all I saw was the cops jumping out of the moving truck that was ferrying them, bees busily stinging them, thinking that they were the source of their provocation. On noticing that our first move was being effective, we emerged with slings and started belting the lorry which at the moment had slowed down as the driver heard the commotion at the back. Seeing us raining stones at the truck, the driver quickly made a U-turn and drove away leaving us hot in pursuit of the cops who were at the moment running after the lorry, waving their hands and desperately attempting to fight the bees which had settled heavily upon them.

With the help of the bees, and the command from my Grandpa, we succeeded in pelting them away. Unfortunately, the majority of us being much younger in age could not keep up with their pace. The cops were too fast for us to catch. One surprising thing - to our dismay - was that none of them upon being stung by numerous bees had even dropped a gun. The other marvellous thing, which I know will be hard to believe, is that none of us was stung by the bees.

It was after about a quarter of an hour when we called of the dogs by giving up our pursuit and withdrew back to the farm quarters. The lorry had stopped far away near the trunk road. It did not take long for the cops on foot to catch up with it.

From afar, with triumphant looks, we watched them board the truck and drive away back to Nondoreet, the district capital, perhaps with swollen faces in which was not at all what they expected. Somehow, I personally felt bad because deep in our hearts we knew that they themselves were being abused by their bosses in order to carry out their wishes. Most of them at that moment appeared miserable and shabby. The majority of them were always clad in worn out boots, patched up trousers and torn sweaters; but we had no choice in our actions, for we had been forced to retaliate.

We believed that this time round they would not have to go and report to the District Administrator manipulating them, but their swollen faces were going to speak for them.

Chapter Twelve

We spent the remaining part of that afternoon harping on about our victory which to us was unique and unheard-of. As it seemed to us, never in the history of the country had cops been beaten off until they had to withdraw by just mere kids who were hardly ten years old, and not more than twenty in number. It sounded somewhat ridiculous and incredible to hear that about thirty cops had been humbled almost to surrender by an army of mischievous boys armed with stone-age weapons and just an old Grandpa who acted as their commander.

That evening, when our fathers and farm men who had not been around arrived, they were briefed about the news of our fearless act by our mothers and my Grandpa. They were somewhat overwhelmed with joy, disbelief and admiration that we had fought back our rivals and succeeded in fortifying our abodes. They hailed us and patted our heads for our outstanding bravery and courage. They told us to keep up the brave fighting spirit and told us that what we had done was highly commendable because we were right.

However, we were reminded that what we had done was nothing but the beginning of a hard task ahead. The act we had shown was automatically going to work up the rage of all the villains of the piece and very soon they were going to come back in full wrath. Deep down in our hearts we knew very well that on the district's head receiving the report of what we had done to his puppets, he was going to fly through the roof there and then.

Another nitty-gritty issue that we that we had to contend with was that we were no match to our rivals in any way. At the back of every mind, there was the consciousness that what we were doing was nothing but fighting a losing battle. The hard fact was that in reality we were not on equal terms with our rivals at all. Deep in our souls, we knew that we were under the feet of mighty men who on their sides possessed law, power and will; men with an excellent network of influence and wearing gold shoes, who could one day, decide to trample us to dust and make sure that our cries would forever remain unheard.

A week ticked by without any sign of another eviction attempt, but we knew that something there at Nondoreet- the district capital - was cooking. They must have been planning and mapping out a method of netting the farm men. This was unveiled very soon.

It was just a week later when they kicked back. This time round they changed their mode of approach

Chapter Twelve

and found us unprepared. It was on the very day that my maternal Grandma had called on us.

The day had drawn in like any other day as the evening gathered very fast. We had homed in to roost for another night, not knowing what the night had in store for us. That night, having been with our Grandma, we turned in quite late, some minutes before midnight.

We had hardly slept for an hour, when screams erupted at the dead of the night which brought every soul to instant wakefulness. We rushed out to be met by a number of strong flashlights. Everywhere was dotted with the lights of torches moving about hurriedly as though impatient to be constantly moving. This sight alone had almost paralyzed every soul with fright as the usual fear-stricken wails thronged the night.

We were still in a state of confusion, looking for somewhere to run when the crack of whips landed on us, making everyone disperse in his or her own way. I clung to my mother who was moving about in a confused state, wailing with pain as my Grandma and Grandpa started to beseech the unknown shadows lashing at us to spare their grandchildren.

'Spare our grandchildren don't kill them!!' Grandpa pleaded in the vernacular at the ghostlike figures with masked faces that were busy lashing at Mama. With horror-stricken heart I wailed in panic as a painful whip lashed my back, which made me let go of Mama and run darting about, whimpering in pain. There was no sign of my brothers. Papa too was nowhere to be seen. This increased my horror further.

'Spare us for the last time,' I pleaded, fear getting the better part of me. Seeing that these men intended to whip us out of existence, my Grandpa had clambered away, while Grandma was on her knees in tears, still wailing for mercy as whips cracked on her, holding my two terrified sisters to her bosom, who were shrieking in fear.

'Pick up the kids and go away you bloody old woman. If you had not been of my own tribe, I would have lashed the daylights out of you,' a strong masculine voice ordered in our vernacular as the speaker dashed away into the next house.

Like a freed sparrow, I made my way tearfully after my Grandma and Mama, who ran slowly, turning back once in a while to check if anyone was after us; Grandma cursing with every step. This time we did not take refuge at the crest of the railway because it too was dotted with the shadowy-masked figures carrying flashlights.

Wails from the people who were being whipped went on thronging the night, as the operation went on. We went with Grandma and Mama, and my younger traumatised sisters, past the small railway leading to the north and stood at the very spot where the ex-chief Arap Kirgit had almost met his fate. We looked back at our homes which to our shock were beginning to go up in flames.

In no time, all the farm houses were blazing in flames, the light of the fires illuminating the night and almost turning it into daylight. Somebody who had just woken up could have mistaken it for a sunrise

Chapter Twelve

at midnight. With the help of the lights, we saw that there was no sign of a single soul within the burning farm quarters but only masked dark figures darting left and right

We watched helplessly as the fire devoured our homes for yet another time. Once in a while you could hear a strong voice amid the wails saying, 'It seems you have forgotten that there is a government in this country. We have come to show you that you cannot outwit us in any way, and anyone who feels he is man enough - let him dare to erect any structure and we will show him pepper.' The booming voice was full of malice.

As the flames of the burning houses got weaker, the wails too died down. Soon everywhere else was dark once again except for red embers flickering on the rafters of the torched homes. The flashlights too had vanished to nowhere together with the shouts of the cops. Despite this, no-one dared to go back to the charred houses, lest they be caught up and dealt with accordingly. We huddled up in the cold night with dry eyes as we waited for daylight to come and reveal that night's abominations.

Dawn gradually shelled us from the pod of darkness in which we had spent the night. Sunrise on the other hand came slowly, as if fearing to expose the previous night's ordeals - the abominable, unearthly and bestial acts in the eyes of God and all people of good intent. We had a hell of time as we fought with ear-biting cold and sharp painful mosquito bites. Our bodies shivered and quaked in the cold, making our noses run. As the sun finally hatched out from the East, we crept dry-eyed to the ring of unfriendly embers and stared at the half-charred remains: a blackened stool, a smashed cooking pot and darkened cutlery and crockery. Clothing and bedding were burnt to ashes, including our school uniforms, leaving us only with what was on our bodies.

Our tormenters were nowhere in evidence - perhaps they had left, perhaps they were lurking within. Everyone was silent as each soul tried to account for the meaning of such miseries, but the meaning was clear and simple – our oppressors were eager to see us quit the farm to give them a chance to satisfy their materialistic greed.

Papa, who seemed to have dodged being netted, according to what we learnt later, was also speechless. Grandpa and Grandma were also turned in on themselves in an utterly dumbfounded state. Mama remained rooted to the spot, her hands on her head. My three brothers, Kiptolo, Kilabat, Kiplumda and I held our small shivering sisters, soothing them as they trembled in the extreme cold.

We never knew how long we remained this way until a fresh masculine wail broke the morning's silence. Everyone turned about sharply just in time to see the old Arap Nyongio kneeling beside his burned house, wailing hoarsely. Literally, it was quite shocking to see an old man shed tears and wailing, for a real African man does not cry that easily.

He was crying, his body rocking as tears flowed down his wrinkling cheeks. We watched him with startled eyes as he scooped two handfuls of ashes. He tightly squeezed his hands and wailed with tears rolling down his face: 'You have always tormented, District Administrator; you send your men to come and pull down our homes, exposing our children to sun, rain and cold as you and your own sleep in comfort.' He groaned in pain, his emotions making everyone melt in tears. 'You sleep in comfort, in your sophistication, as we sleep in the open air at night, feasted on by mosquitoes. Our God in time will hear our cries. You think you are burning our hopes but you are burning yours. Surely I cry out that in the near future, you too will be razed to ashes like these I hold in my hands.' He summed up by throwing the ashes up in air with a gesture of utter hatred.

After this, he slowly rose, picked up his walking stick and walked away, wiping his tears with the back of his hand. As I looked around, his moving words and actions had triggered tears in everyone's eyes. Mama was sobbing, Papa was stifling unshed tears, and my brothers and I were wiping away our rolling bitter tears.

Later Grandma was to leave for our maternal home, taking with her my two younger sisters who seemed extremely shocked, trying to comprehend with their infant brains what was happening. She had decided to do so after convincing my parents that the situation was making them vulnerable by exposure to the unfriendly elements of the weather. They said that, unlike them, we the slightly older ones could easily cope with the situation. We saw them off as tears trickled down our cheeks.

'Take it easy my grandchildren, God is watching. All these things happening will not stop the coming of a new day,' were my Grandmother's last words.

Immediately after coming back from seeing off our Grandma and our baby sisters, Chebusho and Tatamei, we were all summoned by the farm heads. We all sat in the farm's usual meeting ground, inside the spacious wattle trees before the farm's main borehole.

This time round, it was Kipwarir -the headman - who was giving a speech. As usual he looked around solemnly and sadly at mostly women and children, eyeing him with doleful eyes bathed in tears.

'Our beloved wives and children, you are all aware of what is going on. As the headman, I would like to apologize for what has befallen us again; things each and every time are turning from better to worse.

'One thing we have to admit is that we as men of this farm are no longer able to face our rivals. Our forefathers once said that however enormous an elephant is, it cannot give birth to five calves,' he said as elder men and women nodded along with his speech.

'On the other hand', he went on looking around as if trying to notice any mischievous boy, 'you cannot compete with an elephant in urinating because you will end up urinating out your bladder.' He said this humorously as his audience nodded silently.

Chapter Twelve

'Because of this, we are not going to fight back any further,' he said, eyeing where we farm boys were seated, perhaps recalling the remarkable thing we had done just about a week ago.

'From the sources we are hearing now, the District Administrator has sent an entourage headed by the Assistant District Administrator in charge of Loiltorobo Division, which we fall under, to come and confer with us. They are on their way right now and they will meet us gathered right here as we are. We will listen to whatever he has come to say.'

It was ten minutes later when we saw a green jeep and two trucks half packed with cops approaching. We stared as they drew closer, our hearts once again starting to race in fear.

'Do not panic or ran away, let them kill us if they want,' the assistant headman spoke, realizing that some of us were growing jittery.

With darting eyes, we watched the convoy pull up slightly ahead of the farm's main water borehole. The cops poured out of the lorry and formed a semi-circle as the Assistant District Administrator alighted together with the renowned area chief, Mr. Babenyu. The so-called Assistant District Administrator was a paunchy stout man with a dark complexion and a flat nose. His ugly appearance gave a kind of feeling that his mission was malicious.

Escorted by the area chief and five cops, he advanced towards where we were seated, his mouth twisted in a grimace as he rubbed his nose. Upon getting to where we were, he stopped and looked around briefly before spewing out the reason for his visit.

'Listen to me, you wicked Wananchi. I have been sent here by the District Administrator Mr. Chelagat to order you to quit the land before he changes his mind further. From henceforth, we do not want to see the erection of a single structure on this land. We have been very lenient with you but you thrust a finger into an unpleasant spot of the District's head when you attacked the law enforcers,' he said, glaring menacingly at us, his mouth twisted in a malicious sneer.

'I think I have made myself clear. Is there any query before I leave? I have much more important matters of state to attend to,' he said, shrugging his shoulders.

'Sir, we have heard your words but I would like to ask you a favour,' old Arap Nyongio said sonorously, rising to his feet.

'Yes, which favour are you asking for because I do not carry any with me?' the Assistant District Administrator said scornfully, eyeing the old man with detestation.

'Sir, the favour I am asking from you is that since we have no place to take our children to, just please kindly take us to the District Administrator, or tell him to send his cops to come and mow us down together with our children. By doing so, you will have ended our misery,' he said, staring boldly right into the eyes of the Assistant District Administrator who looked quite startled. The chief too looked bewildered by this unexpected statement.

Chapter Twelve

'That is very simple,' he said, after recovering from the unexpected shock. 'We are all now going with you to Nondoreet, where we will carry out your favour, you offensive fool,' he said, signaling the cops to round us up.

'We were all hurriedly loaded into the two lorries. Women and children in one and men in the other. Soon the lorries were bumping away heavily with us towards an unknown destiny. Like oxen being ferried to a slaughter house, we were in a dismal mood, not knowing what was in store for us.

We were about thirty kilometres away, just at the outskirts of Nondoreet, the district capital, when the lorry that was ferrying us unexpectedly ground to a halt beside the road. In sheer shock, we farm children and women were ordered to alight by the cops who were together with us at the back of the truck. They forced us down, some of them kicking and slapping our mothers who were starting to wail in anguish.

When we were all down, the ugly Assistant District Administrator got out of his jeep rubbing his ugly flat nose.

'Now to you women and children, this is the end of your journey; you can see where to go from here. As for your men, you might never see them again,' he said with total finality, signaling the driver of the lorry that was ferrying our fathers to carry on with the journey, closely followed by the one from which we had been emptied.

'Go back home, walk back home,' Papa had shouted, struggling to stifle tears as the cops guarding them tried to silence him with slaps.

With tear-dimmed eyes, we helplessly watched our fathers being ferried away from us, some of them fighting to wave at us that things were going to be alright. I broke down in tears as the lorry disappeared. As the Assistant District Administrator had warned, we did not see them again, not until after a period of nine moons had elapsed.

Chapter Thirteen

With empty bellies and sorrowful looks, and with the help of our mothers, we all struggled our way back home, everyone in a doleful mood. From where we had been dropped by our wicked rivals, it was quite a good distance to the farm. My Grandma having taken with her my younger sisters to my maternal home that very morning, Mama found it an easy task dragging us back home, which appeared like a mirage, about thirty kilometres away to the west.

We finally arrived at our no longer homely homes after trekking for about five hours. Throughout the unpleasant journey, everyone remained utterly speeches as each one of us silently questioned God about the meaning of the trouncing we were undergoing. Each one was dripping with a mixture of anger and fatigue, mouths and throats hot and dry. To our surprise, we found our Grandpa at home attending to the cattle. According to his statement, he had been left after one of the cops begged his colleagues that it was abominable to put an aging man in custody. He had been ordered to go away as we were being herded into the trucks.

Back at the farm our mothers, despite the hard times, managed to make some meals for us. The men had been snatched away from them and left them to fend for their families on their own; temporarily widowed by the men of greed. Life seemed to have turned over a new page, perhaps rolling from bad to worse at the dawn of each day.

There was no ray of sunshine again in the farm which was once very friendly and filled every heart with joy. It seemed that the sun no longer shone on us again for this marked another endless chain of miseries. We spent most of our time worrying about our fathers who, according to what the grapevine told us, had been ordered to be detained in the prison cells without any trial in the court of law by the heartless District Administrator. This was said to have happened in order to allow an important task to be carried out on the land. Anyone prudent could have wondered if an administrator had turned into a judge. But no-one dared raise a finger lest he went the same way.

However, despite the predicament we had been heartlessly plunged into, we were determined to pick up ourselves once again and move on, hoping that the sun was going to shine on us again someday. Our mothers struggled to see that we got all the basic requirements. They went to the extent of selling a few cows and sheep so as to obtain money to buy new household properties after the ones we had before had been reduced to black ashes by the licensed arsonists in the name of the police. We were forced to miss school for a couple of weeks since all our school uniform had been destroyed in the inferno.

It was just after two days when we saw something unusual and unpleasant happening. A section of police officers were brought in and tents constructed inside the railway station premises. As we were still trying to get the meaning of these happenings, a number of land surveyors were deployed to work on the farm's land. After a couple of weeks, our farm had been fragmented into small five hectare plots, but the northern part, which looked like a half of the farm's land, remained untouched.

We only watched from a distance as all these things were being done under the heavy security of the cops that had earlier been deployed into the area. No-one even dared to go near the land surveyors, because they were always guarded by these hawk-eyed policemen who were ever patrolling in a grayish land surveyor's jeep.

Amid this entire goings on, our mothers each and every day, at the crack of dawn, had to travel to Nondoreet to visit our fathers who were languishing in prison remand cells. They had to take them milk in gourds and clean clothes to change into. But the news they brought back every day was quite embittering. They said that from a small window with metal bars, they were allowed to talk to our fathers. They said their eyes appeared bloodshot, sometimes they said they left them while they were weeping, a clear sign that they were being tortured, though they never revealed it even after they were released, for many considered it unmanly.

Despite all these events Mama, with the help of Grandpa, made sure that they gave us hope and consoled us that Papa was okay; because the day Mama had brought news that Papa was in tears, we had all cried bitterly, almost throughout the night. They encouraged us to go to school and study hard because this to them was the only avenue towards the betterment of our tomorrows. They had bought us new school uniforms, text books and exercise books.

Sincerely speaking, our academic potential was outstanding. Ranging from my elder brother Kiptolo, who was at the time in upper primary, to my younger brother Kiplumda, who was at the pre-school, even in spite of us missing school so often, when it came to the end of each term we used to emerge among the top three best pupils in our respective classes. This had attracted admiration from our teachers back at school. By then the majority of them had become fond of us.

'Mama, does God really exist? And if he does, then why does He allow us to undergo all these happenings? Why is he leaving us to the mercies of the District Administrator and his henchmen?' I found myself asking my mother one night while we were seated around the hearth inside a shanty my Grandpa, with the help of Mama, had raised for us to shelter our heads. Mama had stared at me speechlessly as if

Chapter Thirteen

she had not heard my question. I bet she was finding words to answer my unexpected questions.

'God does exist my son. If God was not there, the world could have become a cropper long ago,' she said, eyeing all of us who were staring back at her, my brothers too, eagerly waiting for the answer.

'God has a purpose for you in undergoing all these events, maybe to mould you into humans with human hearts and not humans with bestial hearts in the future.' She went on, 'God created the universe and all that is in it, and created man in His own image on the sixth day.' She said this smacking her lips. 'He gave them the ten commandments, golden rules to govern their behaviour before God and their fellow beings,' Mama had gone on dreamily as we listened with enthralled attention.

'But over the years, selfishness and greed has overrun spiritual powers. The laws have turned cruel and filthy over time, resulting in the present discriminative laws that protect wizards and forbid justice, the laws that prosecute the lamb and set the wolves free,' she finished tearfully, clasping her hands together.

Then all of a sudden she posed some questions to us in that we never expected from her.

'What do you want to be in future?' she asked, pointing at Kiptolo, my eldest brother, who was beginning to drowse.

"I want to be an engineer,' my brother replied flatly.

'What about you Kilabat?' She moved to my second-born brother.

'I want to be a high school teacher,' Kilabat answered thoughtfully.

'And what about you Kipsisei?' She pointed at me, watching me expectantly.

'I would like to be a police boss,' I answered, looking straight into my mother's twinkling eyes reflecting the sparkling fire that was crackling in our midst.

My two older brothers were amused by my answer and eyed me scornfully, but Mama ignored them, moving to our youngest brother Kiplumda, who unfortunately had dozed off.

'Now, I am quite happy to hear that you all have got visions and I urge everyone to stick to his visions to the bitter end,' she said, pointing at the three of us.

'But Mama, Kipsisei's vision is not good, he has to change it. Despite him seeing what the police are doing to us, to the extent of locking up Papa in remand, he still wants to be one of them,' my elder brother Kiptolo said in total protest.

'No Kiptolo, Kipsisei's vision is as good as any vision.' Mama came to my defence.

'As I told you, God has a reason for your undergoing of these experiences. Kipsisei will not in future mistreat others as they do now. Perhaps he is going to mark a new face of the police force. He will stop the cops from being manipulated as puppets and objects for the few evil men of greed, and help them become embodiments of integrity and justice. Or am I wrong Kipsisei?' she asked me, rising up to go out.

Chapter Thirteen

'No Mama you are right,' I replied, feigning confidence.

'So my sons, you will only attain these visions by seeking knowledge from books. Your flapping of pages will one day turn into a massive flapping of wings and like freed sparrows you will fly in a frenzy over the land, calling for the restoration of justice and human dignity,' she said, signaling us to go and sleep as she crept out of the small door of our shanty into a little grassy makeshift, which she had erected for herself to spend the nights in.

After a fortnight our one-time expansive farm land had been reduced to fragments, and new people whom we had never seen started to move in. According to what some had gathered, it was said that the District Administrator had grabbed some fertile land at the south of the district, adjacent to an indigenous forest, brought the owners and resettled them by force in our land.

The northern part of the farmland, which at first had been left untouched, had been fenced with high-quality posts and expensive barbed wire, which was later converted into a double fence. It was almost amounting to the better part of our former farmland. The owner who had taken the lion's share of our one-time land was said to be a millionaire, well known as Mr. Champion. I personally did not bother to find out the field in which he was Championing but I guessed he was perhaps championing the land-grabbing field.

I know that I must have left many wondering what became of the remnants of the crops which had earlier been flattened on the ground. We were denied the right to harvest, since the land has been allocated to new settlers, and had become private property, and just making an attempt to go and harvest became an offence. You could be prosecuted for trespass. Since we had no-one on our side we were forced bitterly to forego everything.

It came to our realization that it was because of all this, that they had decided to detain our fathers and other able-bodied farm men. It is quite clear to many that no man with a sound mind can withstand seeing his only means of livelihood being snatched away in his very presence and fail to fight back.

So with very little that we could do about it, we just had to stand aside with pent-up anger and watch the embittering miseries unfold. I felt that we were sailing inside small boats that for their survival must always strive to keep to the shore and let the larger ships venture into the deep sea.

Chapter Fourteen

As the days ticked by, things went on turning from bad to worse. At the crack of every dawn, despair and depression came together. As if they had joined our rivals to embitter and make our already miserable state more miserable, each sunrise came along with its contribution. In other words, predicaments were no longer raining but pouring.

First came the talk of an outbreak of a dangerous disease spread by mosquitoes which medical experts had termed 'Highland Malaria'. Over the radio, we had heard each day of new cases of the disease, which was said to be spreading quickly like wild fire in a dry savannah. Escalating death tolls attributed to this blood-curdling malady were reported.

These unsavoury reports came as totally unwelcome news to our ears. Having been exposed to the severe elements of weather and a handful of mosquito bites, we were an outstandingly obvious target and a good home for this deadly disease to make a roost. This blood-chilling fact gave us a kind of feeling that this nasty epidemic was tailored and well-calculated to come and further our misery. It was probably coming to cash in and make a good home out of our present situation.

'Talk of the devil and he will certainly appear,' our Grandpa used to warn us. Indeed I agreed with his words when the much talked about and most dreaded fever reported its arrival in the farm. I am not ashamed to admit that I became the first victim to be knocked down by this parasitical disease. I did not understand why it chose me as its first target but I guess that maybe I was somewhat less immune to it.

It was just in the middle of the morning lessons at school when I suddenly came down with a nasty body-quaking fever which made my body seem to blow hot and cold simultaneously. This was seconded by a splitting headache that made me whimper, writhing on the ground in pain. This commotion drew the attention of our cheerful class teacher whom we had nick-named Mrs. Good. She quickly left the books she was marking outside the door of our classroom and ran to my rescue. She lifted me to my feet as she tried to inquire about what was ailing me but out of the sheer pain I was unable to answer. I only doubled up holding my head as the paralyzing pain throbbed through it.

On realizing the state I was in, she had quickly fetched my elder brother Kiptolo and another elder

Chapter Fourteen

pupil in his class to take me home. With difficulty, they took my hands and led me home. In every step I felt strength failing me as my body joints ached, making my feet fail to respond to my will. Upon my brother and his friend noticing this, they gave me piggybacks in turns.

By the time we reached our no longer homely homes, the headache was giving me hell. It was as if my head had turned into the forge of a mad smith who was hammering it tirelessly. To our disappointment, Mama was not at home. She had left with the other farmwomen to commute to Nondoreet, the district capital, to visit our fathers in custody. Grandpa too was not around; he had taken all the farm livestock to graze in the government's department's land. This is because our one-time land was now strictly out of bounds.

So my brother Kiptolo and his friend left me to the mercies of our immediate neighbour, Tiebo Songhor, and went back to school. The old woman attended to me by giving me some aspirins and wiped my temple with a cold wet piece of cloth, perhaps to reduce the escalating body temperatures.

At around ten in the morning, I was no longer myself. I was shivering beyond words, and sweating profusely. The headache too was not giving me even a slight break, it was hammering even more than before, making me double up in pain, writhing left and right on the grassy ground. For the first time in my life, I thought I was about to die.

On the old woman noticing my situation worsening, she made up her mind to give me a piggyback to Naseru Rural Health Centre, which happened to be about four kilometers to the south. She lifted me to her back and carried me up and down the railway line and picked a meandering path which was a sort of bee-line short cut to the health facility.

With every step, I could hear her heaving heavily as I dangled on her back. By then, I was seven years old and I thought I was slightly heavy for her. Once in a while, I would hear her murmuring to herself and cursing at an invisible being.

'God, if you have elected to kill our young ones, then give us a land to bury them, and if you aspire to sustain them, then shower them with rains to wash away the galling bitterness that has been already embedded into their tender hearts by these senseless men of greed,' I heard her say loudly as she lowered me down in the cool shade of a big tree. She was probably tired and wanted to have a breather.

We arrived at the Health Centre some minutes to noon but to her distress, there happened to be no drugs. There were a multitude of unattended patients lying everywhere in the compound, who too seemed to have been left stranded. Tiebo Songhor lowered me under a small tree and left for the Health Centre premises, perhaps to look for any means of my being attended to.

'Mr. Elder Statesman's government has failed us in everything. In fact I wish the white man was here to stay. We are being taxed but not being catered for,' I overheard an aging man conversing with a young man with a small sprouting beard who too seemed to be annoyed and disappointed, having brought in a patient, who looked like his mother, only to be told that there were no drugs in the facility.

'I totally agree with you Mzee,' I heard the young man admit. 'If the white man was here, we would have been attended to even at our homes by mission medical experts, but look out now, we face an unknown destination,' the young man lamented bitterly, lines of anger written on his face.

'We bestowed our country's resources and treasure on these so-called great men with high hopes, not knowing that they were another breed of blood suckers, hyenas dressed in sheep's clothing, cannibals who turn and eat up their very own, their own blood. Oh God, send us your Messiah,' the old man added bitterly.

'They are busy bringing down the country to rack and ruin. They are shamelessly and recklessly looting the treasury leaving only an empty shell for us,' the aging man lamented further.

'That's one of the Africans' weaknesses: they say that you cannot look after a communal cow without milking it,' the young man put in once more.

'They say so but I totally disagree with that outmoded belief. I sometimes try to concur with them, but I have failed to buy their idea. They are overdoing the whole thing. They have over-milked the cow to its knees, leaving its calves to the mercies of starvation.'

Despite the paralyzing pains I was in, my subconscious mind managed to hang on every word of their moving conversation. I found myself aligning with their words. To my surprise, hot tears trickled down my cheeks, and the reason was not the pain that was ailing me.

'God must intervene where men are defeated,' were the last words I heard from the latter before I was picked up by Tiebo Songhor. She wordlessly lifted me on her back and made her way back home as I dangled on her back.

When we were halfway home, she suddenly broke into a psalm, which she movingly hummed as she struggled with my weight.

*'Unto thee I lift up mine eyes, o thou that dwell in the heavens. Behold, as the eyes of servants look unto the hand of their masters, and as the eyes of a maiden unto the hand of her mistress; so our eyes wait upon the Lord our God, until that day He will have mercy upon us. Have mercy upon us, O Lord have mercy upon us: for we are exceedingly filled with scorning of those that are at ease, and with the contempt of the proud,' s*he lamented, on our homeward way.

Without any medication, we arrived home in the late afternoon. We found Mama already at home. She was in shock when she learnt that I had received no medication, despite the bad condition I was wallowing in.

'What an endless chain of misfortunes, where is our fair share in this world?' Mama lamented bitterly her eyes raised to the skies.

'Weep not child, there is no oppressor that oppresses non-stop. The misfortunes might have

Chapter Fourteen

trailed us like tails but this does not stop the coming of a new day,' Tiebo Songhor consoled Mama whose eyes were getting moist.

'God himself will know what to do with our children; everywhere we go, we get no help. Their fathers are languishing in detention and the authority seems determined not to set them free at all soon'.

'My child, together we are in this, we have to accept our present state and thank God in every situation we are in. Let us keep our chins up and let things take their own course. Above all let's hope for the best because the man above knows why we are undergoing all these troubles. In time, He shall hear our prayers, look down and shed a tear upon us,' the old woman consoled her further.

After my mother's effusive thanks, the old Tiebo Songhor made for her makeshift structure made of dry maize stalks and grass. Mama placed me under a castor oil plant right beside our jerry-built home. Once in a while she would come to check on my temperature with the back of her hand and then resume her house chores. The remaining part of that day went on sluggishly. Time seemed to take a slow pace as though to prolong my pains. The pains thronging my head went hand in hand with my pulse. By the time the day eventually came to a close, I was no longer myself, I was wallowing in intense, unimaginably severe fever.

On Grandpa arriving with the cattle from the grazing fields, he was shocked when he saw the state I was in. Without taking a breather, he took out a hoe and a machete and disappeared into the woods across the railway line. He later came back with roots, leaves and barks of certain plants. He ordered Mama to boil them before compelling me to gulp down a cupful of the galling soup. The bitter and nasty soup derived from the so-called medicinal plants made me tipsy, triggering nausea.

In a minute, I was retching madly like a sick dog, my hand on my throat, as I spewed a galling yellowish and greenish chime. This led to a complete loss of appetite. My four siblings were all there, watching me, pity being the only thing they could afford to offer me, sometimes giving me a cup of water whenever I asked for one. That night I felt like eating nothing though I could feel pangs of hunger gnawing my innards. I wallowed in this state till a heavy slumber pitied me, taking my consciousness away, praying to be in good fettle the next day.

My hopes of coming out of the deep sleep feeling a bit better were dashed when I woke up to find out that I was much worse than before. I had grown so weak and weary that I could hardly stand. I felt completely off-colour. Grandpa's nature cures seemed to have failed to work and in turn made me frail.

The situation took another turn when many people at once joined me in the world of ailment, my brothers Kilabat and Kiplumda among them. They had just arrived from school for lunch break when they too came down with the menacing fever, each complaining of intense headache, and aching muscles and joints.

Chapter Fourteen

The issue almost outweighed Mama's strong courage, putting her in a daze, not knowing what to do. But she bore it bravely. I could not help admiring her courage and determination as she moved about with her daily house chores and nursing us on the other hand. Once in a while, she would strip and mop us with a cold wet cloth whenever she felt that our temperatures were escalating to greater heights.

As our lovely neighbour old Tiebo Songhor had said earlier to Mama that together they were in this, her household was struck too by the same fever. Her two grandchildren, Chemaiyo, my classmate, and Chemptai who was still quite young, joined us in the victims' world. Others in the rest of the farm were Tapwago, the wife of the Old Arap Nyongio who had been reported to have convulsed on several occasions and later went into a coma. Neither were my friends Kipronyei and Kipsiya spared by the epidemic; they too had been struck down, turning the entire farm into a nursing home.

'God, spare me so that I can nurse my children, and attend to their father in detention,' was Mama's recurrent prayer, especially when she saw the situation worsening.

Up to this moment, His Excellency Mr. Elder Statesman's government had not even shown any effort to keep the fever's outbreak in check. This made the outbreak gather momentum, striking almost everybody down in the region. The district capital Hospital Wards were reportedly said to have carried thrice their capacities of unattended malaria patients, but startlingly enough, the government had not batted an eyelid over the issue.

Fingers of blame were pointed, and accusations from human rights watchers and clergymen were once again being leveled at Mr.Elder Statesman, blaming him for the situation. Funnily enough, The Father of the Nation in turn turned an accusing finger to his Minister in charge of the Ministry of Health, saying that he was sleeping on his job. The Minister of Health blamed the Minister of Finance for not allocating enough funds to his ministry, which he said was running at a deficit. As if that was not enough, a vicious circle of blame kept on, the Finance Minister accusing back the Health Minister of frittering money away on imaginary projects and needless expenditure. Cornered, against a wall, the exasperated Health Minister let fly at doctors and nurses. He alleged that they were hoarding and channeling the government's drugs into their private hospitals and clinics.

However, the paramedics from non-governmental organizations and mission hospitals left the top dogs raving and blaming everything on each other. They rushed in to save the situation, as they too kicked up a heated fuss over the credibility of the government. The famous Catholic Mission Hospitals in conjunction with foreign mobile doctors came in and set up mobile clinics in the region. People on receiving the reports thanked God for those, mainly foreigners, who unlike the politicians seemed to have human dignity at heart.

Chapter Fourteen

These doctors came and put up a mobile clinic inside Naseru railway station premises. Mama received the news of a medical expert's arrival as God's answer to her ceaseless prayers. She cheerfully ferried us in turns on her back to the venue.

We were attended to by white doctors assisted by black nuns, who were happily attending to hordes of patients, cheering them up and reassuring them that they were only curing them but that it was God who truly heals. We were all given a dose of one painful injection in our bottoms and three big rounded tablets.

A couple of days after receiving medication, we started to pick up, a sign that our frail bodies were responding to medication, something which made our weary Mama and Grandpa bubble over with joy. My emaciated bony body started to put on some flesh, covering my already protruding bones and ribs, which before could be counted under my only oversize blue-black striped shirt.

In a week's time, everybody had fully recovered, though the after effects of the epidemic were still in evidence in some people's bodies. People who had escaped, uninfected by the malady, including my elder brother Kiptolo, Mama and Grandpa were given some oral preventive tablets, something which these medical experts had termed was a sure way of acting as a final nail at the coffin of the malady. By the time the paramedics were decamping, saying good riddance to the malady, quite satisfied that the vicious outbreak had been curbed; a good number of people in the region were reportedly said to have died. Fortunately enough, nobody in the entire farm and its vicinity had succumbed to death from this deadly malady.

Chapter Fifteen

'After every storm follows calmness,' some say.

'In every predicament, there is a droplet of relief,' our teachers used to tell us, but unfortunately there seemed to be none of the above so called wise sayings that corresponded with our lives. It seemed that every fortune had shut its doors on us.

As I have stated earlier that it seemed every misfortune was calculated to deepen our misery, there followed another epidemic which reduced our lives to destitution. We had hardly forgotten about the horrific Highland Malaria when our livestock came down with a strange disease that ended their lives within a day.

At once, many of our cattle and sheep were lying everywhere heaving, saliva dripping and their one-time smooth hair ruffled. Our mother struggled to look for veterinary services but all was in vain. Grandpa, who was a staunch believer in natural cures, tried to treat them with herbs but that too came to nothing.

In two days' time, the majority of our cattle were dead. There were several carcasses scattered as the disease took its toll among our only remaining means of livelihood. We tried as much as we could to curb the malady from spreading by both burning and burying the carcasses, but as the days went by, more animals died till they were too much for us. We ended up leaving the carcasses to rot away as we watched.

In one week, out of our fifteen head of cattle, one bull, twelve cows and a heifer, there was only one cow that we had named Tuimet and her heifer remaining. The rest had succumbed to the disease which had made them bleed from all the openings in their bodies before breathing their last.

This distressing thing wore out my mother's hope and made Grandpa Sulk. It was an unbearable thing which plunged everyone into a state of hopelessness. There were very few cattle which had survived in the entire farm. Kipwarir's twenty herds of cattle were all gone, a third of Kipeng'eng's dead. The only person who seemed lucky to be left with the biggest herd was old Arap Nyongio. About a half of his cattle remained untouched, perhaps because the majority of them happened to be indigenous breeds.

When our mothers took the bad news to our fathers in custody, we heard that they nearly flew through the roofs of the prison cells in which they were being held. Papa was said to have broken into tears, Kipwarir wailed and Kipergeng collapsed.

Chapter Fifteen

We could not help feeling for them for we fully understood the predicament they were in. On top of that, they were said to have become emaciated, something which reflected the ordeal that they were undergoing.

'These tests of time seemed to have been tailored to eradicate us up to the hilt,' Mama said to Grandpa that very evening after arriving from the district capital where they had gone to convey the odious news to Papa.

'Mmmmh.' Grandpa had only heaved a sigh; his wrinkling hands on his aging face.

'Imagine - they have not let us harvest our crops, which are rotting un-harvested in the fields; the food reserve is running out, only two sacks of corn remaining. To cap it all, the disease has wiped out the entire herd, leaving only Tuimet and her heifer. What is next, beyond starving to death?' Mama went on as Grandpa listened in silence.

The agony in Mama's voice was quite embittering. It was very true that in the next three weeks or so, we could be starving to death right in the midst of the land of plenty. I personally hated myself for the first time, hated the farm's heads whose ignorance had plunged us into our predicament, hated the District Administrator and his contingent of cops, and hated the so called Mr. Elder Statesman for being naive about what his subjects were undergoing. For one more time I felt murderous feelings rush into my heart and I felt like reaching out for the throat of each of our oppressors. Our future so far seemed to be dangling in the balance, quite uncertain, but we felt we should at least kick our last before we gave up.

That week was followed by some dramatic events which, if their intentions could have materialized, would have triggered another lethal feud. The first of them was to do with Grandpa. There was a certain man known as Charles, who was one of the cops who had camped inside the railway station to provide security for the land surveyors who were almost through with fragmenting our one-time land. He was one of those strict police officers and he used to patrol frequently along our makeshift shelters, making sure that no one had re-erected a reasonable building.

How this cop fell for Grandpa's trick was funny. If Grandpa had been well conversant with his gun, this Charles would have been no more. It was said that Grandpa had entered into a conversation with this cop, telling and retelling him his numerous stories about the many battles he fought while he was serving in the Colonial Army, some of them being during the North African Campaign, the Battle of Alam Halfa, the Tunisia Campaign and the Battle of Medenine among others. Charles had become more enthralled with Grandpa's tales, oblivious of his motives. On Grandpa's noticing the cop's vulnerability, he had dashed forward and toppled the cop off balance, snatching his gun in the act, turning the muzzle towards the startled cop, trying to pull the trigger on him. But poor Grandpa, having got used to the old manual guns, ones used during the Second World War, could not efficiently operate the modern automatic rifle. The cop was reportedly said to have bounced back with the dexterity of a cat and snatched back his rifle pushing Grandpa off balance and hitting him with the butt-stock of his gun twice on the chest, before taunting and kicking him severely.

He left him to roll on the ground groaning and cursing. This episode had happened amid the jeers of the people around. The cop was said to have sneaked away back to the camp in shame after being jeered at by a growing crowd that had threatened to lynch him. Kiptolo who happened to be within, rushed to lift Grandpa up to his feet as a string of curses bubbled out of his mouth.

'These idiots deserve to be killed. I assure you that if they do not vacate here very soon, I will make sure that I die with one of them,' Grandpa had said as he struggled to recover his breath, every so often coughing and holding his heaving chest.

'I have lived the better part of my life and I will not care if I have to spend the remainder in incarceration,' he had vowed, fully determined to carry out his threats.

It was after this dramatic event of Grandpa attempting to shoot the cop when some elder boys hatched out a plan targeting Mr. Champion, the man who had taken the lion's share of our one-time land that stretched northwards. This plan happened to be one of the last kicks in our undying string of struggles.

The intelligence we had gathered on our own had it that every evening, Mr. Champion would patrol around his newly-acquired giant tract of land inside his white Land-Cruiser pick-up driven by his white manager, whom we had heard called by the name Lukas. We had decided to set a trap to lynch him to death, which to our surprise he managed to fall into, only cheating death by a whisker.

Our aim was to find a way we could lure Mr. Champion inside our farm quarters where we could teach him the lesson of his life. We were all determined to eliminate him because we felt that this was the only way that our cries might be heard. To us, justice had become a dirty word long ago and when justice turns into a filthy word, hatred, violence and death remain the only viable options. Diplomacy had failed and violence was the only possible thing in fighting for our rights.

That very afternoon without letting anybody, including our mothers and Grandpa, know of our intentions, all the elder farm boys had played truant, dodging going back to school for the afternoon lessons. We sent out Kipronyei and Kipsiya as scouts into the railway station to check on the movements of the cops in their Camp. By this hour, the land surveyors had retired to Nondoreet where they were based.

We re-grouped ourselves inside the bushy shrubs ahead of the farm quarters as we waited for the scouts to bring their feedback on the whereabouts of Charles and his colleagues. We had gathered our double-pointed sticks, boulders and slings including two machetes which were with Kibelat and Kiptolo.

Chapter Fifteen

It did not take long before our spies, Kipronyei and Kipsiya, rushed back heaving heavily with excitement.

'There is Charles alone in the tent, the rest have walked to the south, and I hope they have gone to hunt for illicit brews,' Kipsiya had stormed in breathing heavily.

'That's good, Charles alone is nothing to us - we can deal with him. If Kiptolo's Grandpa humiliated him by himself then he is nothing but a dose of salt to us,' Kibelat, who was one of the eldest among us, assured us smilingly.

After making sure that the coast was clear, we sneaked away towards Mr. Champion's land. Slightly to the east, there were some houses of the new settlers being erected, others almost ready to be moved into. So far, the new settlers who had been resettled in our one-time land had not moved in except for two families who had camped nearby to put up their homes. One of them was a tall ebony old man with balding head and graying hair, with a very large family. They had noticed us as we raced northwards, for they all stood perplexed, following us with their eyes, but we did not mind much about them.

On arriving at the edge of Mr. Champion's land, we descended upon it by bringing down the double expensive fence by the use of the two machetes. We destroyed the eight strand barbed wire fence by winding it with the help of the droppers, as we watched out for Mr. Champion and his white manager to come on their usual afternoon patrol.

We had just brought down a good portion of the fence when the usual white Land Cruiser pickup appeared across the main trunk road that divided Mr. Champion's land in half. In the distance, it stopped and we saw Lukas as usual climb to its roof with his binoculars and he seemed to have immediately got a sight of us. He had quickly descended and in no time we saw the pickup truck accelerating at a high speed in our direction, the vehicle rising and falling along the bumpy field.

We gave them time to draw closer before we broke into a small run, retreating slowly and tactically towards the farm quarters. On arriving at the scene, they abandoned the vehicle at the very spot where we had destroyed the fence and made after us on foot. To our glee they happened to be both present, Mr. Champion and Lukas, his white manager.

It was at this time that Tapsaga, Kiperng'eng's wife who was attending to her only remaining she-goat, caught sight of us. Being a sly and tricky woman, she quickly shouted at us to take cover inside the shrubs as she advanced forward to meet the perspiring Mr. Champion and the said Lukas, who happened to have closed in on us. Within a fraction of a second, we were nowhere to be seen. Like chicks acting upon the warning of their mother hen, we had hidden ourselves in the shrubs, lurking and waiting for Mr. Champion and his manager to walk into our trap.

'What is wrong, Mr. Champion? What have these bloody little brats done to you?' We heard the cunning

Tapsaga confront Mr. Champion who was burning with rage, his hands thirsting for our blood.

'Mama, imagine - they have destroyed my fence; wait until I get my hands on one of them, I will skin him alive,' Mr. Champion replied in an angry vengeful tone.

'Calm down Mr. Champion and follow me, and I will show you a room where they have hidden themselves. How can such mischievous brats toy with the property of the most renowned world champion who has brought our republic of Kalyaland to fame by winning numerous gold medals! No! This can't happen while I watch!' Tapsaga uttered cunningly as Mr. Champion and his Lukas followed her, unaware of her ill intentions.

Inside where I had taken cover, I could not help smiling at the vulnerability of Mr. Champion and his white manager who could not uncover the sly cunning of Kipeng'eng's wife. Like a lamb being led to the slaughter house, he followed Tapsaga who was by then busy beckoning him to go after her, unaware of our intentions to lynch them into the past tense.

After walking past us, oblivious of our presence in the bushes, Tapsaga all of a sudden brought down the house by yelling out a quick calculated shriek.

'Uuuuuu! Uuuuuu! Here is Mr. Champion - he has brought himself to us; let's kill this land grabber, maim him!' was Tapsaga's message.

We all dashed from our hideouts aiming for the heads of our startled prey as Tapsaga got hold of them. With the speed of lightning, we descended upon them with boulders as they struggled to free themselves from Tapsaga's strong grasp. With the most desperate moves of ones who have smelled death, they struck Tapsaga off balance and made off for their dear lives, with us in hot pursuit, pelting them with the boulders and the double-pointed sticks. Unfortunately for them and fortunately for us, Lukas the so called manager, tripped over a stump landing on his belly as Mr. Champion escaped by a close shave.

We gave Lukas a terrible beating till his white skin turned pale before he managed to escape. We went on after him as he yelled out for help. His nose was bleeding and his face swollen.

'Spare the white man and go after Mr. Champion,' I heard somebody yelling out as we went after him. We gave Lukas a chance to escape, shifting our target to our main culprit, Mr. Champion, but the man was too fast for us, something which gave as an idea that he was not only a champion in the land-grabbing field but he was indeed a one-time world athletic champion.

We gave up our chase when the two got into their truck and sped away to safety, perhaps to seek medication and report us to his colleague, the District Administrator.

As we withdrew back into our quarters, we could not help ourselves laughing to tears, as we replayed the incident in our minds. To someone who could have been watching, it was somewhat ludicrous to

Chapter Fifteen

see such a world-renowned champion being beaten by a handful of kids, hardly above ten years of age. We gave no thought to the repercussions our act might trigger. They had detained our fathers, brought down our homes, flattened and denied us our crops and so far we had nothing to fear because we had nothing at all to lose. We were altogether hard up, over and out. In our minds it was 'Come what may come.'

However, there followed no kick-back: Lukas was said to have straightaway booked a flight-ticket to his motherland in the name of seeking medication, but this poor innocent victim of circumstances never made a come-back.

Chapter Sixteen

In every Desert of Calamities, there is an oasis of hope - so goes the good adage, but to people of our kind, such consoling words seemed to have distanced themselves from us, for they sounded far-fetched.

Our lives entered into a nasty chapter of destitution, misery and want. In a fortnight we were all crawling in abject poverty. Our food reserves had run out, something which reduced us almost to panhandlers. Many a time we were forced to miss school, so that we could spare time to go and labour in the neighbouring farms in return for meals.

The mid-year heavy cloudbursts too cashed in on our misery to dampen our predicament further. We had nowhere to shelter and no-one to turn to but to wait upon the impartial super human said to be dwelling high above, perhaps to send us manna, but unluckily it seemed that we had totally fallen out of His favour. The cold associated with these heavy rains made us numb, for we did not even have warm

Chapter Sixteen

clothing to cover ourselves. Our shanties and makeshift houses were leaking terribly and in no time it was even preferable to stay outside instead of inside for they had turned muggy and damp.

As the days went by, we grew more wistful, completely down in the dumps. We eked out a living hanging on the grace of those who happened to be in possession of human hearts. Our mothers were forced to go and labour in people's farms, determined not to let us go hungry, but most of the time we were forced to do without midday meals, sometimes taking wild green vegetables for supper.

At this time, a lot had happened and more was continuing to take place. The land surveyors had wound up their work after allocating our one-time land to the new settlers who were by now beginning to move in, in full swing. The cops-Charles and the company who had camped inside Naseru railway station, for the purpose of providing security to the surveyors had also decamped, abandoning us desperately struggling to keep afloat amid the tumultuous waters of the troubled time they had wholeheartedly plunged us into.

Amid all this, there were unpleasant ordeals which were taking place in Kalyaland's politics. The already muddy political arena seemed to be getting muddier. This time seemed to be a season for dangerous talk where obsequious political veterans, afraid of political reform, had turned into loose-tongued men advocating violence, determined to keep the wave of change at bay so as to preserve their cronies.

Many such politicians had been cited making irresponsible and implausible statements, even in the most severe possible taste and without regard for any substantiation. Most of this had to do with the disquiet on the part of some politicians about the demand for reform in the country through the national multi-party calls. A good number of powerful politicians realized that they had a great deal to lose if major reforms, along the lines being proposed by the public, could come to fruition.

Moreover, these efforts of the politicians and government in power in their attempts to crack down on multi-party advocates seemed not to have stilled the waters. Instead they were followed by several days' rioting in Loilrobi, the Kalyaland's capital, and other principal towns, among them Sisimuka, which was a volatile lakeside town in the west. These had caused His Excellency Mr. Elder Statesman's government to use a free-hand, by involving his police officers to quell the chaos, something which seemed to have worsened the situation, resulting in many fatalities. These men in uniform had nothing like 'basic human rights' in their vocabularies, handling their victims senselessly with excessive force and wanton torture. This was however not surprising to us because we had already experienced the sting of their wrath in our own backyard.

Then there was a famous controversial cleric known as Bishop Felix Gemu, a diocesan bishop in charge of Nondoreet Diocese, who also, it seemed, had stood against all the odds. His sermons had many a time and more hit banner headlines due to his criticism of Mr. Elder Statesman's government and his undying cry for justice.

More often than not, he had erupted with a bang as he rose up against inequality and tribalism. Apart from calling for justice in the political arena, and more restrictive checks on corruption and land grabbing, he had attracted the attention of the masses by saying that a clique of powerful cabinet ministers had formed an impenetrable ring around the Father of the Nation, and that they were gradually cutting him off from the people of Kalyaland by constantly feeding him with false information and giving him bad advice. He had gone on to list a host of misdeeds revolving around corrupt practices allegedly perpetrated by powerful politicians and senior civil servants, mainly the District Administrators, demanding a commission of inquiry to probe into such activities.

He had also walked the extra mile, telling politicians to their faces that they were not in their political positions through the mandate of the electorate but that they had rigged themselves into power. This alone seemed to have taken the piss out of the politicians, for they started to pour scorn on him, others openly threatening him with death. The regional politicians flayed this great clergyman and described him as an agent of foreign masters who were bent on wrecking the beautiful country of Kalyaland.

But these political and clerical wrangles had no place in our minds. We were just beginning to hear about this Churchman who seemed to have continued to draw media attention with his charged and highly controversial sermons and statements on both clerical and secular issues. So far, we had enough miseries to occupy our minds as we battled with impending starvation and the cold weather. It was at this time that we got a report that our fathers had finally been released from detention. Upon this great news coming through, we received it with mixed feelings, although we were elated at this happy reunion after fatherly love being snatched away from us for a period of nine moons.

They all of them arrived that very evening. We ran to them as tears of joy uncontrollably coursed their way down our cheeks. They all looked out of sorts, emaciated and weary. They were no longer the fathers we used to know. Papa had lost a great deal of flesh and looked wearier. However, he managed to put on a smile as we clasped him elatedly. Mama's emotions were infectious; she had broken down and sobbed so much even after Papa assured her that he was still okay. Grandpa too had hard time trying to stifle back his tears but the agony in his voice betrayed him.

'My son, they thought they would take you away from me, but you are here to stay. After the cruel hand of death snatched away your brothers from me, leaving you alone, I went down to my knees, offered a sacrifice and begged God earnestly to protect you. Nothing will harm you my son,' Grandpa said sobbingly amid tears. 'Nothing will bring you to harm,' Grandpa went on, hugging him.

Chapter Sixteen

To Papa, the misery he had found us in seemed to be too painful for his tears; he only put on a pensive face, once in a while wagging his head in disbelief. The nine months' detention seemed to have distanced him from reality and he was always in the doldrums.

A lot had happened while they were locked up in prison on remand without being tried. They seemed to find it hard to come to terms with the reality. The land they had left un-fragmented now stood totally different. It had been allocated to people whom we never knew. The large herds of cattle they had left behind had all died and the cattle enclosures displayed emptiness throughout.

'These bloody people have entered into partnership with the devil to barter away humanity,' Papa had only muttered, his non-twinkling eyes fixed on our emaciated bodies.

Before even Papa rested to let the odour of prison remand blow away, he was already on the road the next day on a borrowed bicycle to call on his old friends and distant relatives with the intention of looking for something for us to put into our bellies. He seemed to have gritted his teeth and decided to come to grips with our predicament.

Some well-wishers too who seemed to have been touched by our unpleasant state called on us, one of them being our usual visitor, cousin Truphosa. She had worked hard and shown that she was truly a relative indeed. Every day, she would share with us whatever little she could afford.

But life itself seemed to have decided to play hard on us. I am saying so because two days after Papa had been released from the nine months' incarceration, Mama came down with a strange illness which remained a black spot to us. She was ever complaining of body-aches and hardly ate anything, a thing which made her already hunger-ridden figure deteriorate further.

Papa bore the situation and took charge of the house chores with the assistance of my two elder brothers, Kilabat and Kiptolo. Papa had succeeded in finding us some food which though little, at least gave us some energy, which propelled us to school and back. Having earlier been brought up in a state of plenty, we had a hard time trying to acclimatize our bellies to appreciate the little meals they got. Another issue was that having grown up accustomed to plenty of milk; we now had to take plenty of water which we substituted for milk.

One striking thing, however, is that despite all these bad conditions, Papa was very strict on us about missing school. To reward him, we were always determined put a smile on his face. To be sincere, the end of term academic performance on our side was superb. In spite of our going to school sometimes without breakfast and coming back home in the evening to the makeshift structures which we called homes, all four of us emerged the best pupils in our respective classes.

'Well done my sons; if there is something that has given me hopes to live on, then it is because of you.

Chapter Sixteen

Work hard and never relent, though the dark heavy cloud of hopelessness may hide your stars from you, it will one day vanish to usher in the days of joy and prosperity,' Papa had told us patting our backs, his face depicting extreme happiness for the first time since he had arrived from detention.

Our happiness was however short-lived when Mama's state of health worsened, forcing Papa to seek assistance from my maternal uncles who came and took Mama to the district capital hospital where she was hospitalized. The diagnosis revealed that she was suffering from depression which had resulted in stomach disorders. She was said to have started developing stomach ulcers.

We however thanked heavens for keeping Mama healthy to attend to us while Papa was still away in custody. With all these predicaments, there was very little we could do about our situation. We had no option but to sit on the whirlpool waves of taunting life, embracing each other for comfort as we watched and prayed for an answer.

Chapter Seventeen

Whoever uttered that every dark cloud is accompanied by silver lining, seemed to have had our situation in mind. In a week's time, we were called on by an unusual visitor who resuscitated our dying hopes, giving us a new lease of life, an event that gave us a kind of feeling that our ceaseless cries had eventually attracted God's attention. It also seemed to signify that out of millions of people who had witnessed our plight, only one of them seemed to have been touched, and it gave us a further feeling that he was truly a God-sent messiah.

It all happened one Sunday evening while I was sitting by the farm's bare road, watching my mates play about. It was the same day that Mama had been discharged from the hospital bed and brought back home. Her health had slightly improved but she was still in total distress.

As usual, I was in low spirits as I struggled with hunger which was perpetually gnawing my innards.

Chapter Seventeen

We had gone without our midday meal that very day and the fate of the evening meal was not yet known.

I had cupped my cheeks with both hands, eyes fixed on my fellow farm children to whom life seemed to be normal. I had slightly tilted my glance when my eyes caught sight of two white vehicles purring their way at a moderate rate along the farm's main road towards our homes. The vehicles comprised a small white saloon car which was blazing the trail, closely followed by a white mini-bus, which in those days was informally known as a '*combi*'.

Immediately, the entire farm was on its feet watching the advancing convoy, others beginning to panic. Any sight of vehicles earlier before was a sign of misery but this time, judging from the way they were approaching, one could tell that they were not malicious as the others we had witnessed before - for they looked more like those on a peaceful or a humanitarian mission.

In no time, they slowly came to a halt some few metres away from where I was standing still. Soon the occupants were out and it did not take long for anyone to recognize that they were nothing but clergymen. One of them was a man in a bishop's collared shirt and black suit, with a chocolate complexion, much hair, smooth face and big pair of glasses.

All of a sudden, there were whispers all over as people drew closer to him. 'It is Bishop Gemu! Bishop Gemu!' the elderly, including Papa and others, started whispering to one another. This name alone made me realize that our impromptu visitor was no-one else but that most renowned controversial cleric, Bishop Felix Gemu of Nondoreet Diocese.

For some strange reason, he did not utter any word for a while. Ignoring the wondering looks and the whispering, he only moved around inspecting our homes. He stopped next to Tiebo Songhor's shanty, took off his glasses, wagged his head in disbelief and turned around back to us, blinking his eyes which seemed to have turned moist. We were startled to see him weeping.

He reached for a handkerchief in one of his pockets and wiped tears away and put back on his spectacles before signaling to one of his companions who had a camera to go to him.

'Mr. Wafula, take a photograph of each and every family in their respective shanties. I want the District Administrator and president to come and tell me whether these miserable beings are not citizens of our beloved republic of Kalyaland. How can you evict people, burn their houses, destroy their crops, expose such innocent tender children to unfavourable elements of weather, then come and resettle strangers in their own land? No! This cannot be, this is injustice of the highest order and it can only happen over my dead body.'

Bishop Gemu had fuming anger written on his face, fresh tears starting to well up in his eyes; something which brought our misery home to us. To many, they know perfectly well that a true African man does not shed a tear that easily.

Chapter Seventeen

Soon, Mr. Wafula was busy taking photographs as directed by his superior. Others, who were in the Bishop's entourage, comprising two cheerful ladies, were moving about patting our heads as they conversed with the elderly. We fetched our ailing mother and we were all photographed together. The two ladies seemed to have noticed that she was not very well, for they immediately came and took hold of Mama's hands.

'What is the trouble with you Mama? Are you ill?' they asked, eyeing her already emaciated figure with pity. Mama had only nodded, struggling to go back to her bed which was just outside our shack.

'Have you got medication?' they further inquired with deep concern.

'My children, she has just arrived a few hours ago from the hospital,' Grandpa intervened.

'Nothing will harm you, God is here for you and we are here for you too. God will heal you,' the two ladies re-assured Mama as she finally got to her bed. One of them just left for the vehicle and came back with a carton which contained some rice, cooking fat, maize flour and some beans.

'Take this, Father. The patient must have something to eat.' They handed the provisions over to Grandpa who in turn thanked them effusively.

'Thank you my children, God will reward you, your treasure is in heaven,' Grandpa said emotionally.

'No, it is our duty to help those in need; we will bring you more relief food tomorrow to see you through as Mr. Bishop battles for your rights,' the two cheerful young ladies assured him. We later learnt that they were the Bishop's personal assistants. They then introduced themselves to us and gave us their names. One of them, who was rather short and light in complexion, was Ms. Rachel Moraa, and her companion, who was slightly taller and darker, was Mrs. Arnodha Tiebor. Papa and the rest of the farm men were among a crowd that had gathered around Bishop Gemu who was busy questioning them and taking notes. We later learnt that he had taken the names of the family heads and our number in total.

When the bishop was through with collecting and putting down every detail which he had gained from the farm heads, he summoned us before him as he eyed us wistfully, his eyes expressing a mixture of anger and pity. When we were all there before him, he cleared his throat before he started speaking to us.

'Children of God, I was just passing by and I decided to come here in person to see the situation for myself. I have been moved by your miserable state and I don't think that God is happy either about the whole thing,' he had gone on adjusting his glasses. 'I as the servant of God am here in this world to voice the voices of the voiceless, teach people the will of God and preach the Gospel wholeheartedly. I will work hard to make sure that you get back that justice which you have been robbed of. In the meantime, the diocese will send some relief food for you tomorrow. My last message to you is that you pray without ceasing, for it is only from God that we can seek refuge and solace. Furthermore, He says in His good book that 'If you abide in me and my words abide in you, then anything you ask for will be given you.' Let's bow our heads and pray.'

We all solemnly closed our eyes, heads bowing as he began to pray loudly with vigour. One amazing thing is that up to this very moment, I can still vividly recall every word of the prayer he said.

'Our heavenly Father, above all kingdoms and authorities,' he had started, as people nodded along with him. 'I call upon your name this hour of this day. God, Jehovah, Father, listen to our prayers, and shed a tear upon these miserable children of your kingdom, Lord. You know the misery which they have been plunged into by men of greed. Almighty Father, listen to the cries of your oppressed children. They are crying for justice and they have no comforter. Power is on the side of their oppressors and they have no-one to turn to. Our heavenly God, melt the hearts of their oppressors. Those gluttonous men move boundary stones out of sheer greed, they pasture flocks they have stolen, and they drive away the orphan's donkey and take the widow's ox in pledge. They thrust the needy from the path and force all the poor of the land into hiding.

'Like wild donkeys in the desert, these poor people go about with their children. They gather food in the pastures and glean in the fields of the wicked. Lacking clothes they go naked at night, they have nothing to cover themselves in the cold. They are drenched by mountain rains and hug the rocks and trees for shelter. God, we have lost sight of your glory but we are not destitute souls, we are still able to wonder that you carefully made us in your divine semblance. We believe that you will listen to and answer our prayers because you are a faithful God, and not one that lets his people down. I do pray and believe in the Holy Trinity,' he summed up his touching prayers, as everyone shouted: 'Amen!'

Upon lifting up our heads, everyone's eyes were moist. Bishop Gemu and his entourage got back into their vehicles and drove away the same way that they had come, waving to us that they were going to be back soon. We happily waved back to him, without the foggiest idea of whether we might ever see him again.

The following morning, as they had promised, they sent a lorry with relief food comprising yellow maize flour, wheat, cooking fat, salt and packages of sugar. As we received the relief food that very day, a twinkle of hope and happiness in people's eyes that had vanished long ago, was back with fresh glee and gusto. Once again, life was bustling afresh in our hearts as everyone prayed and urged God to keep on holding us.

Chapter Eighteen

Hope plays an important role in human life and it is the last thing that man can lose. I am saying this because after being visited by Bishop Gemu and assured that he was going to fight for our cause; our dwindling hopes seemed to have been rekindled. The glee which had vanished from people's faces had come back, and once again there seemed to be a fresh sunshine in our faces. This made us realize that one man with courage is a majority in himself.

As Bishop Gemu had promised us, he was said to have headed straight to Mr. Elder Statesman's high palace where he displayed the photographs before him. Bishop Gemu, being one of the human rights and justice crusaders, was said to have taken Mr. Elder Statesman to task, showing him that he was without doubt failing in his duties as the Head of State.

From what we heard, Mr. Elder Statesman was said to have turned mad with fury. He had rung our District Administrator's office where he got him on the line. The district's head, Mr. Chelagat, on being asked about the issue, had absolutely denied everything, saying that the people he had evicted were occupying land belonging to the government Department of Defence, something which was a complete lie, because our one-time land was not part of the government's land but only bordered it.

These barefaced lies seemed to have infuriated Bishop Gemu beyond words. Determined to prove them wrong, he travelled back to Nondoreet, our district capital, where he was said to have exchanged bitter words with the District Administrator, openly accusing him of being one of those who had entered into partnership with Satan to barter away humanity. The District Administrator then started to warn him against tarnishing his excellent leadership and good reputation.

Furthermore, Bishop Gemu being adamant came back with his camera and photographed the concrete beacons that marked the border between our one-time land and the government's land. He then went back to Nondoreet where he proved the perfidy of the wicked district head before heading back to display his evidence before the head of state. His Excellency Mr. Elder Statesman seemed to have been finally won over by Bishop Gemu, because he was said to have immediately ordered the tyrant in our district capital to give us back our land. This he promised Mr. Elder Statesman to do so as soon as possible.

'Your wish is my command Sir,' the District Administrator had assured Mr. President.

Chapter Eighteen

The valiant Bishop Gemu was reportedly said to have given the District Administrator an ultimatum to give us back our land or else he was going to make sure that the whole world would get to know of his evil behaviour

With revived hopes, we had started cheering happily for this man of God, in whom we saw a true picture of a humanitarian. We were once again optimistic about going back to our happy long-gone days and that very soon things were going to be as before. We were looking forward with great expectation to regaining our dignity and having back the justice we had been denied by these evil men of greed.

Our gaiety and hopes went to a higher notch two weeks later, when we discovered that the newcomers who had been settled on our land had stopped moving in, while others were starting to remove their building materials. However, there happened a fatal event which nipped our hopes in the bud, an event which was a terrible blow to our new hopes, plunging us back into a pool of hopelessness and mute shock. It also indicated to us that everything had chosen to go against us.

The heart-breaking news that altered our lives at that point came through one fateful evening when Bishop Gemu was said to have travelled to Asibu, a border town located in the western part of the republic, to attend a mass which in other words meant that he was going to look into a statement by a prominent but loose-tongued cabinet minister. This cabinet minister, serving in Mr. Elder Statesman's government, and known as Honourable Mang'ondu, Minister for Manpower, was one of those politicians who had now and again threatened those who were advocating good government with death. He had earlier told Bishop Gemu that he would not leave alive if he ever stepped into his political backyard.

Honourable Mang'ondu's reckless talk, however, had come at a time when not only he but many of the republic's politicians had decided that it was an open period for barking forth careless and dangerous statements. Most of it had to do with disquiet on the part of other politicians. Clergymen, one of them being Bishop Gemu, and majority of the public seemed to have joined hands to demand reforms in the country, an issue which made these few rigid politicians such as Honourable Mang'ondu to see them as a threat to their political existence.

The wicked, savage and blood-curdling news reported that our beloved Bishop Mr. Felix Gemu had died in a tragic road accident on his last journey home from his trip after conducting a massive open air service in Asibu, a border town in the west. The farm and entire region was plunged into a state of mute shock as news of the calamity spread. Soon, the dumb shock ruptured into mournful wails as the people in anguish tried to come to terms with the horrifying news. As for us, we couldn't believe our ears. We could not believe that the only one among the millions who had offered to champion our struggle to get justice and our rights back was no more.

Chapter Eighteen

I personally was not able to put up with the issue. I broke down just beside our shanties as hot tears burst out of my eye sockets. I could not believe that the man who had offered us food and hope, as well as promising to fightfor our cause, was no longer alive.

'Wuuuuwuui, wuuuuwui! They have killed him; they have killed him, the one that gave us hope to live on!' Tapwago, Arap Nyongio's wife, had hysterically wailed her hands on her head as she rolled on the ground, mad with grief.

Everywhere was filled with tears and wails as the wicked news sank despairingly into people's minds. My ailing mother, who had slightly recovered, broke into sobs, her body quaking;all my brothers were in tears, Papa and Grandpa silent, their hands on their heads. Kipwarir, Kiperng'eng and Arap Nyongio among the other men were fidgeting about, walking here and there in disbelief, some doubting the credibility of the horrendous and unpalatable news.

Tiebo Songhor was no longer herself; she was running about to and fro, screaming terribly in a high note which left many almost deaf.

'You might have killed him, but you are not yet at your destination for you have not killed his soul and his good works!' Tiebo Songhor had yelled at an invisible being, darting about in intense grief.

For sure, the entire farm seemed to have lost its head as the sounds of loud mourning thronged the air. It seemed as if the entire farm quarters were crawling with invisible beings that were moving about, lashing at everyone with invisible whips. A startled crowd as usual had formed up on the railway crest watching the entire drama, others thinking that we were mourning the death of one of us, only to learn later about the death of Bishop Gemu.

The implication of Bishop Gemu's untimely death left a lot to be desired in our minds. According to a press release from the international media, Bishop Gemu had left Asibu town where he had made a victorious visit at about noon that fateful day, after conducting a massive open air mass. His visit was said to have brought the town to a virtual halt as locals and workers abandoned their tasks to join in the celebration-like conduct of the mass. Leaving Asibu, Bishop Gemu was driving and had three passengers in his car, two of whom were identified as Ms. Rachel Moraa and Ms. Arnodha Tiebor; the two cheerful young ladies who had offered us a carton of foodstuffs on the Bishop's last visit. Three other cars carried the rest of his entourage who were, together with Bishop Gemu, advocating political and judicial reforms. The Bishop took the long way round, skirting Sisimuka, a major lakeside town in the western part of the country next to Asibu, before emerging on to the main Kivulwe-Nondoreet road.

It was shortly after passing Kivulwe, near Loiltorobo market on the ultimate lap towards home that Bishop Gemu's car caught up with a wide-load long truck moving in the same direction. Coming from the opposite direction was, reportedly, a fuel-ferrying track, freewheeling down the steep incline

Chapter Eighteen

while incessantly hooting with its headlamps on. The wide-load long truck was reported to have rubbed the trailer with its side before slamming into Bishop Gemu's car and dragging it some distance, and then overthrowing it as it was released from its metal grip. The entire force of the crash showed that the truck's front spindle was ripped off and Bishop Gemu's vehicle reduced to a twisted wreck, that had to be forced open with steel bars in frenzied attempts to free the occupants. Bishop Gemu was found dead, pulverized between his seat and the steering wheel. His three passengers, including Ms. Rachel Moraa and the caring Arnodha Tiebor, sustained serious injuries and were rushed to Nondoreet district capital nursing home.

By now, suspicions were widespread, chiefly concerning the politician's apparently clairvoyant utterances coming true in sinister fashion. Some said it was Mr. Elder Statesman's government plot to eliminate him, others emphasizing that his death was stage-managed by our ruthless District Administrator, Mr. Chelagat.

Earlier on, in an intuitive statement released by Bishop Gemu before he left for Asibu, reacting to Honourable Mang'ondu's warning against him venturing into to Asibu, which was the minister's backyard, he had said that it was just the prelude to a scheme to have him exterminated.

The following morning came Gemu's victorious but ill-fated entry into Asibu, followed by the catastrophe, after he had already left his opponent's backyard, and was only a few minutes' drive from his Nondoreet base. The first reaction was one of mute disbelief and rude shock. The politicians' earlier utterances had certainly served as fodder breeding suspicion of foul play. This had in turn placed Honourable Mang'ondu and Mr. Elder Statesman's government in a somewhat perilous situation.

Further press reports indicated that the Bishop met his death a few hours after his visit had stirred the border trading town of Asibu to something like a wildly restless state. On his arrival in Asibu, he was reported to have gone into a small social joint for refreshments which was within minutes beset by enthusiastic locals, fervently urging him to address them in a local stadium. Being one of the renowned controversial clergymen, he had walked from the said social joint at the head of continually-growing crowds to St. Paul's Parish Church, where he was said to have preached a sermon based on his familiar themes circling around the pressing need to re-institute justice, and singling out land-grabbing, corruption and the flawed electoral system as major shortcomings that must be corrected. During his mission to Asibu, which ended up by being his last mission on earth, Bishop Gemu was said to have taken the opportunity to criticize the cabinet minister of manpower, Honourable Mang'ondu, warning against the pitfalls of loose talk.

'A tongue is a small part of the body but it can burn the entire nation,' he was reported to have said.

Chapter Eighteen

That fateful night, we ate nothing and did not sleep a wink. An irreconcilable grief and anger battered our hearts. We were back in the tumultuous rough waters of gloomy grief as hundreds of fresh fears of the unknown poured into our already weary and shrunken hearts. Death had crashed in and wiped out the only one who had stood up for our cause, sending us staggering back into destitution. The earlier wailings and loud mourning had calmed down into a deep silent grief.

Later that night, Mr. Elder Statesman sent out a message of condolence over the radio. The Head of State had words of praise for the late Bishop Gemu's contribution to national issues, singling out his contribution to social justice in giving a voice to the voiceless poor. He assured the family of the Bishop that they were all grieving together in that period of sorrow.

Some termed Mr. Elder Statesman's message of condolence as nothing more than a mouthful of hypocrisy and that he was shedding crocodile tears, where the eyes are crying and the heart celebrating, perhaps for the thorn in the flesh which has been finally dug out by accidents of time.

The following morning we joined other people who had lined up along the trunk road to view the wreckage of Bishop Gemu's vehicle being towed to Nondoreet. With deep sorrow, we watched the mangled wreck of the Bishop's car, in which he had visited us in, wrapped in a white cloth drift away past us as fresh tears stung our eyes.

Chapter Nineteen

It was a fortnight later, when Bishop Gemu had been buried during a well-attended funeral thronged with a multitude of mourners, weighed down with grief. All our parents, including our recovering Mama, travelled to Nondoreet to pay their last homage to this great man of God who had died – and with him our hopes. The burial was said to have been attended by a number of dignitaries, headed by His Excellency Mr. Elder Statesman. Some were said to have collapsed, foes shedding crocodile tears and friends crying out in genuine weeping.

Never before had the death of a Bishop been mourned by the entire land, but Bishop Gemu's death had aroused suspicious feelings in hearts of those who knew him well. Many could not imagine that his death had robbed them of their protector. In the aftermath of his death, we recoiled into our previous

Chapter Nineteen

cocoons, our faces masked with a fresh fear, for we had no idea what had been kept in store for us by our wicked rivals. Now that the one who had stood up for us was no more, we knew that we were certainly waiting for more unpleasant things.

It was about a week after Bishop Gemu was buried, when our fears were confirmed once more. This time we received an unexpected visitor whom we had only been hearing about but had not yet seen. It was the so-called District Administrator, the heartless tyrant who was one of the shadowy forces fuelling our misery - Mr. Katwa Chelagat.

He arrived some minutes before noon, escorted by a fully armed party of eagle-eyed security personnel comprising his well-known Admin Cops and the blue-clad General Duty Police. We knew his mission was malicious and that he had come to mock, taunt and scorn us.

As they alighted, no-one ran away, we only watched as the cops dispersed to cover a wide area, before the District Administrator emerged from his white state- owned jeep and summoned us to go near him. He was a young man perhaps in his early thirties, with a slender figure and dark complexion. His wide mouth was always twisted in a permanent grimace.

When we were all there before him, he watched us with disdain, his wicked mouth degenerating into a lopsided smile depicting contempt before emptying it.

'You wicked people of this land; I have come here in person today to meet face to face with you who have proved to me over time to be stubborn and rude,' he had started, without even a greeting.

'Yes, I must admit that you almost outwitted me but now I have had the last laugh. No-one on earth can defeat me and my will. Anyway, to be brief, I have come to notify you that you are still supposed to clear off from this land as soon as possible. I do not care where you will go but my message is short and clear: I do not want to see you here again. You sent your clergyman to harass me before my bosses, but he is no more; maybe you can go and resurrect him from his grave.' He wound up his wicked and ruthless speech then vanished into his jeep. In no time he was speeding away together with his henchmen.

With stunned looks, we watched them drive away, everybody wagging his or her head in disbelief.

'Some people were created purposely to perpetuate malice and torment others,' I heard Papa telling the old Arap Nyongio, who was lost for words.

'But his days on earth are numbered. He has committed the un-committable, disgracing God and his people,' Arap Nyongio had replied to Papa in a downcast tone.

Despite all these hard times we managed to carry on with life. The relief food that had been donated to us by Bishop Gemu before he died ran out, returning us back to our previous state of famine. Out of sheer hunger, we children started operating like vagabonds, sneaking in and out of neighbouring maize fields. Because anything looks palatable when death by starvation is imminent, we started feeding on raw tender maize cobs and chewing fresh maize stalks. We never cared what we ate as long as we could feel that it was going to postpone the untold hunger that was perpetually gnawing our innards. Sometimes we could be tempted to steal green corns from the far neighbouring farms and move far away into the woods to the south, where we could roast and eat them to our fill. However, we did this without the knowledge of our parents since they abhorred stealing and had they found out of what we were doing behind their backs,would have handed out some severe beatings.

The new settlers who had shown signs of leaving came back in full swing to erect more houses; others, the likes of Mr. Champion and other top officials in Mr. Elder Statesman's government, putting up sophisticated complex mansions and mansionettes, which dampened our hopes further.

However, there was a fearless act carried out by Mama and Tapwago, the old Arap Nyongio's wife, a thing which made me feel that misery and denial of justice can drive someone to do something suicidal, a thing unheard-of. I do not know how Mama and Tapwago had got hold of the report that His Excellency Mr. Elder Statesman had jetted into the western part of the country and would be travelling back by road to spend the night in Nondoreet, our district capital state lodge.

Mama and Tapwago had that afternoon girded their bellies with *legetiet* - locally made broad leather belts, used by mothers to gird themselves after birth. This to many looked absurd and strange because it was unusual. They then left towards the main trunk road running to the west, ostensibly to look for wild vegetables and mushrooms for our supper. We had no idea that they were intending to do something which earned them the titles of heroines of the day.

According to the reports that we heard later that evening, Mama and Tapwago had survived by a whisker from being run over by the presidential motorcade. They said that on the arrival of Mr. Elder Statesman's convoy, that mostly comprised all his cabinet ministers, Mama and Tapwago had dashed forward and knelt right in the middle of the road, making the presidential motorcade swerve off the road in the attempt to avoid running over them.

'Father of the Nation, we are being killed and tormented, we no longer have anyone on our side. They have grabbed our land, we no longer have shelters and our children are going hungry,' Mama and Tapwago had cried out, holding their broad belts high in the air, weeping before Mr. Elder Statesman's motorcade which at the moment had so unexpectedly ground to a standstill.

It did not take long before Mr. Elder Statesman's guards and henchmen came out and recklessly dragged Mama and Tapwago off the road to let the motorcade move on. However, Mr. Elder Statesman did not show his face but left, perhaps shocked, abandoning Mama and Tapwago to regain their composure at the roadside where they had been roughly dragged, weeping bitterly.

Later, before they came back home, one of the presidential guard was said to have been sent back to inquire about what had made the two women do this most unexpected thing. The black-suited guard had interrogated Mama and Tapwago who earnestly explained their grievances to him, which he wrote down in his notebook. But out of sheer shock before he left, he threatened Mama and Tapwago saying that they were lucky to be alive.

'You are very lucky you stupid women, thank God, because by now you could have been no more, you could have been met by this,' he had said, drawing out his pistol and showing it to the faces of our still sobbing mothers.

'As for this,' he had said, displaying his note book close to Mama and Tapwago's tear-dimmed eyes, 'it will not reach His Excellency, because I will distort it'. He spoke with scorn, and we later came to know him as one of those who had benefited from our one-time land, and was among those who were erecting mansions to the East, having got a big chunk of land.

That very evening, as the news of Mama and Tapwago's valiant acts spread, a string of excited farm members came to our makeshift house to express their joy and to congratulate Mama for her fearless act which must have startled our rivals. Mama and Tapwago remained heroines in people's eyes as other farm women sided with them. Among them was the old Tiebo Songhor, Tapsaga and Magdalena,

Kipwarir's wife who could be seen moving around them ululating.

Later on that night, word of mouth was sent by the regional chairman of Mr. Elder Statesman's ruling and only party, Mr. Tembwo, saying that their cries had been heard by the president of the republic and that he wanted to meet the women and their children in person at our district capital state lodge very early in the morning the following day, before he left for his palace of palaces that was situated at the heart of Loilrobi, the country's main capital.

This message made our excited Papa, Kipwarir, Kiperng'eng and other farm men go and look for a vehicle to ferry us to Nondoreet the next morning, for an important appointment with the head of the republic.

With great expectation and anxiety everyone, on receiving this great news, began to bubble over with a mixture of happiness and anxiety. The next day we all woke up at the crack of dawn before the eastern horizons was even bleached by the breaking of the new day. We were told to clothe ourselves in our navy-blue school uniforms before we boarded the waiting pick-up which we believed would ferry us to meet Mr. Elder Statesman in Nondoreet's State lodge, anxiety biting everyone's feelings. The journey to Nondoreet to us looked eternal, as if it was a journey into space. Each one seemed not to be able to wait to meet this big man who had power to channel the misery out of our lives.

After an hour, we were already approaching the town as the sun emerged in the east with the vague image of a smiling face. Everywhere was draped with national flags and standards of Mr. Elder Statesman's ruling and only party, which in other words symbolized the presence of the highest authority in the land. We were dropped together with our mothers at a point which was some distance away from the State Lodge. Before the vehicle left, Papa and the other farm men whispered some instructions to Mama, Tapwago and the other farm women whom we were left with. After the vehicle had left, we slowly walked besides the road heading to the district capital State Lodge under the strict supervision of our mothers, most of the children clinging to their hands.

As we walked, the town was slowly coming into wakefulness as hordes of hurrying humanity hit the roads. The weather was a bit chilly but the nip of the cold air was dispelled later as the sun gained more strength. There were some men busy planting and tying flags along the roads, others climbing up the electricity and telegraph poles to tie the national and ruling party flags high above the towering poles.

We had walked for some minutes when a police car suddenly appeared from behind. On catching up with us, it slowed down and cautiously herded us along, before they ordered us to branch off and head towards the town centre, telling us that they had organized our meeting with the Head of State at the District Administrator's office which was situated in Nondoreet's town centre. After this, the car sped away ahead of us.

With bated breath we walked close to our anxious mothers, as we waited with great solicitude for something to happen. We had reached a certain roundabout, when three jeeps descended from nowhere. In no time we were all rounded up by blue-uniformed police officers and ordered to board the three vehicles. I knew what it meant and did not wait to find out. Out of great fear, I shot off shrieking in a high note and took to the streets. Mama struggled to reach out for me but I was already gone. With my heart in my mouth I dashed about the streets in terror and confusion as two policemen ran after me. I nearly brought the entire town's traffic to a standstill; two vehicles missed me by inches, which resulted in a series of mild collisions. I gave the police officers a hard time as they tried to get hold of me, as bystanders and passersby briefly stopped to watch the drama of cops versus a tiny kid in school uniform.

Whatever had made merun away was not a mere fancy, but an imagined idea of where we were being taken. Many a time I had heard stories of people who had been detained in police cells, one of them being our father, something which had instilled great fear into my heart. For whatever reason, I knew their mission was not a good one. In ordering us to board those police vehicles, their plan was to lock us up in the cells, a thing which I could not put up with.

It was after frenzied attempts to find a place to hide when I ran into the feet of a tall man with thick boots and jungle green starched trousers. He caught

Chapter Nineteen

me in a mighty grab and lifted me up as I screamed now and again while trying to bite him, struggling to free myself. When I looked up at him, I recognised the figure immediately. He was the ugly figure of that cop who was in charge of the men who had severely demolished our homes.

He carried me towards the still waiting jeeps as the other two blue-uniformed ones reached up for me panting heavily.

'You silly thing, you have given us a hard time out of sheer mischief. Just you wait - you will face pepper,' they had said, as they started to work on me. They severely pinched and slapped me as they escorted me towards the waiting vehicles. At this time, I was busy screaming for help and at the same time struggling to regain my breath. Upon reaching where the vehicles were, they carelessly hurled me inside where I crashed into Mama and the other women who were still struggling to fight back.

But we were soon overpowered and they ferried us into the Nondoreet Police Station where we were forced down, stashed into cells and locked up. The muggy, stained and dark cells choked our breaths with an unbearable stench of urine and all manner of human waste. Everyone was looking about in great astonishment and disbelief. Our hopes of meeting with the head of state at that moment seemed to have been dashed. It was very clear that our opponents could not allow us to meet him lest they be caught out. So they had resorted to locking us up to avoid our meeting him at any cost.

We hopelessly and helplessly stared and wallowed inside the dark cell for a long time. At lunch hour, we were brought a semi-cooked mixture of maize and beans that was pushed inside under the door by an invisible being. We tried to eat it but the disgusting stench made us sick.

We stayed this way for hours conversing in low tones. It was late in the evening when we heard the sound of hurrying footsteps along the corridor coming towards the cell. On reaching the cell door, the sounds of the footsteps stopped and we heard a jingle of keys before a key was inserted into the key-hole and the door knob turned. The door opened and a figure in plain clothes peeped in.

'Oh my God! What is this I am seeing?' he said, trying to scrutinize us. 'Are these not women and school children?' he said to himself, turning round.

'Sergeant! Where is Sergeant Kibirech?' he called out in a loud voice.

'Sir,' replied a deep voice.

"Who locked up these school kids and women in the cell?' he shouted, anger written on his face.

'It is the District Administrator who ordered us to do so sir,' the potbellied sergeant replied.

'Get out! Get out! Who is this who wants to ruin my job?' he yelled out at us, fuming with anger. We later learnt that the person who was barking out the orders was the officer in charge of the police station who had apparently happened to be away when the entire drama took place, and upon arriving had decided to conduct a routine inspection of the cells, thus finding us.

Chapter Nineteen

We poured out through the cell door, squinting in the light that was coming in from outside. Just outside the gate were our fathers secretly signalling us to get out of the gates. Papa was there looking around as we were herded towards the gate. When I looked at the sun, I could tell that it was some minutes past five in the evening.

'Ah! Ah! Ah! Are these the ones who wanted to meet the father of the nation? Go now after him, he is not far away, he just left some minutes ago, and you might catch up with him,' bellowed one of the cops, as we eventually walked out through the gate. We ignored his scornful utterances as Mama eyed him with detestation.

We met Papa and other farm men outside the gate where they were waiting beside the vehicle which had ferried us. Just looking at them was enough indication that they were a worried lot. I tried imagining the ordeal they had undergone while in detention, bearing in mind just the few hours which we had spent in the cells. I could not imagine what they felt because if just spending a few hours in the cells was so detrimental to us, what about spending a whole whopping nine months in such a state? At this thought alone, I felt my eyes welling up with tears of pity.

With melancholic hearts, drooping shoulders and bereft of hope, we slowly boarded the waiting pick-up van. We knew and felt that there was no fair share for us in this world. We were fighting the battle of haves and have-nots in which the eventual winner was obvious. However, this humiliating act happened to be the final nail in the coffin of the many attempts we had employed in our pursuit of justice.

Chapter Twenty

With bruised and shrunken hopes, we went back to our unwelcoming homes completely out of sorts. We were already crawling in abject poverty and barely thriving, for we no longer had anyone on our side that bothered to fight for us. The only one who had stood out for our cause had been removed from the face of the earth; an issue which had put our lives on the receiving end of further torment.

It is said that in a state where there is no hope, people cast off all restraint. This immediately came to happen, for it did not take long before confusion and misunderstanding hit the farm. The farm members started to quarrel amongst themselves and chaos became the order of the day. The two barbaric sons of Tiebo Sohnghor cashed in on the chaos and perpetuated it. They turned against Jackton Kipwarir and his assistant Jethro Kiperng'eng, demanding to be given back the share they had been contributing towards the acquisition of the farm, saying that the sheer ineptitude on the part of the farm heads was a major cause of the entire predicament.

They went to the extent of assaulting Kipwarir, causing him to lose two of his upper front teeth. After this, they stripped themselves to their birthday suits before invading the home of Kiperng'eng, where it resulted in a bloody fight. They slashed and taunted one another with machetes, something which almost led to the loss of lives. Josiah was hacked on the head and Faruk, Kiperng'eng's eldest son, struck unconscious. These chaotic incidents marred the farm, causing the previous screams and wails to come back into our lives. We were no longer fighting our usual adversaries but each other.

And it came to pass that when the whole country was beginning to wallow and sink into a hideous maelstrom of ethnic feuds, incited by war-like politicians that we left the farm's chaotic quarters and moved into an uninhabited place at the easternmost part of the farmland, next to its border with privately owned lands.

The politicians who seemed to be afraid of political and constitutional reforms, led by His Excellency Mr. Elder Statesman and his cronies such as Honourable Mang'ondu, were busy moving all over the country advocating tribal violence. They were openly sowing and watering acres of negative ethnicity. They planted forests of tribalism. They fostered ethnic hatred, which triggered the fatal and infamous ethnic feuds that yielded the fruits of vengeance and death.

Chapter Twenty

'Clear the bushes that have encroached upon your homesteads. Let us no longer allow the fleas to jump up and down, dancing the *Sendeiyo dance* on our soil,' were their calls. This anger and hatred planted over the land yielded prickly leaves, which wounded people's hearts, causing the sores of malice and negative ethnicity to fester. Houses were torched, and people slashed and tormented one another, sometimes to death, because of ethnic hatreds. The law enforcers moved in to try to avert the impending ethnic cleansing, and in some parts they succeeded in quelling the chaos, but in other areas they seemed to have been overwhelmed.

Amid all this, we moved and settled in a relaxed and quiet place where we hoped to make our hearts settle and live at ease. Our parents seemed to have felt that we had been brought up in enough violence, cruelty and detestation, that we had undergone more than our fair share of the world's malice. We had had a bellyful of all these sorrows and it was high time that they thought carefully and looked forward to the tomorrows of their young ones, fostering high hopes for our education, since they were already heartened by our academic promise. I thought it was high time for them to remould our characters that had endured the unbearable - the environmental conditions excellent for nurturing future notorious hardened and radicalized criminals- and rehabilitate us to live in an environment of honour, virtue, and the rebuking of vice. Earlier on, they had begun attending Sunday Services at a nearby church and ensured our attendance at the Sunday school run by the same church. Later on I came to understand that they had made the decision to make this a turning point and had dedicated their time to pacify our hearts that had been bred up to violence, and instead instill in us the fear of God, and replenish our spiritual bankruptcy.

As I recall that very day of departure, as we carried our few remaining belongings on our heads, I could not help myself shedding a tear. The place we left behind was a place where we had shed the most tears of our lives and I believe that the soil up to this very moment must still be bitter with our tears. It was a place where we cried a great deal, tears flowing in torrents, but unfortunately our cries fell on deaf ears. Our weeping was like the proverbial fish sobbing, where their tears are always carried away by water and forever remain unseen.

At the country's top level, the political storm had quickly gathered momentum, triggered by the introduction of a multi-party system. The previous famous and tireless clamour for constitutional reforms in the republic of Kalyaland that had earlier been ignited by the late Bishop Felix Gemu and those of his opinion had come to the boil and yielded fruit that had let off the steam of the masses. These events seemed to have given the so-called unbeatable head of state a hell of a time as he had been pressurized by both internal and external demands for him to ditch his loyalty to one party state and let the people of the country have a say through what they termed as democracy, government by the people and for the people.

In time, Mr. Elder Statesman was said to have submitted to the pressure, letting the people to have their own way. For the first time in the history of the country, people were granted the freedom to express themselves and to freely vote for their preferred presidential candidates in a secret ballot. The detained political prisoners were set free out of the torture chambers, and they too cashed in to make capital out of the already free political arena.

At that time, my elder brother Kiptolo was approaching his final primary national examination in our republic of Kalyaland, later to be followed by our second-born brother Kilabat the following year. Despite all the terrible happenings we had gone through, both of them had maintained a high academic performance. This seemed to have further heartened Papa and Mama's spirits who saw this as the only future for us.

The first ever political campaigns were associated with election violence, which surged through our republic of Kalyaland. Many lobby groups formed to campaign for the re-election of Mr. Elder Statesman to lead the republic for yet another five-year term, and they were busy moving about dishing out money and other baskets of goodies in an attempt to woo the electorate to vote him back.

'Please we beg you. Give Mr. Elder Statesman another chance. Let him complete the development projects he had started,' his campaigners were urging.

'No, tell him to go to hell, he has failed us in all aspects of life,' his opponents were replying.

'Yes, he might have failed to deliver but let us give him another chance. Mind you, a cow might have four legs but that does not guarantee it from tripping and falling over,' his advocates had called back.

'No, we have had a bellyful of his dishonest and wicked leadership and his corrupt government that favours the rich. We will replace him, he is no longer part and parcel of us,' others had said.

'No, please, give him another chance, look at his development records. On top of that he is one of us; he is our own blood, our tribesman. Furthermore, even a badly-decayed rat with rotten manners does not cease to be a member of the rats' family,' they beseeched further.

'No, a bad and rotten rat with un-ratty manners should be discarded and cast into the abyss of no return where he will be forgotten for good,' the advocates of change barked out.

'These people advocating change are speaking the truth,' Grandpa had told Papa one evening when he had just arrived from bringing back our younger sisters, Chebusho and Tatamei, from our maternal home.

'Yes they are right; Mr. Elder Statesman's government has failed the hardworking people of our beloved republic of Kalyaland. He has outlived his usefulness and is excellently ripe for a replacement,' Papa had replied, looking straight ahead into the

Chapter Twenty

field, where the tender wheat crops of neighbouring farms were fluttering in the evening's rustling winds.

In the long run, the elections were held later in the evening of that very year, when Mr. Elder Statesman had a landslide victory, trouncing his opponents in the election marred by rigging allegations. This victory came to our ears as another bitter pill to swallow, which meant it was yet another five-year term of misery. Mr. Elder Statesman was sworn in as the father of the republic of Kalyaland for yet another period of half a decade.

Strangely, since then I have found myself developing a great aversion towards Mr. Elder Statesman and his government in general. Even when it came to the usual moments of being ordered at school to rush and cheer him at the famous junction on his usual tours, I started dodging into the maize fields or malingering to avoid seeing him. I personally found no reason for going there to shout myself hoarse, singing worthy praises to this unworthy great man with a heart of stone. A man who was so ignorant of what his subjects were undergoing. Even more galling was that despite two women running the risk of losing their lives by being run over by his endless string of motorcades, by blocking his way and crying out for his intervention, he never bothered to make a follow up. He had fallen prey to misinformation from the clique of powerful and greedy politicians who were busy enriching themselves at the expense of the voiceless.

****
****

More than two decades have passed since we lived through those evil times. Millions of gallons of water have flowed under the bridge, but nothing has happened so far. Despite all this, I would like to spell out clearly that I harbour no ill will towards our former oppressors or bear any malice as they go on wallowing and munching mouthfuls of their ill-acquired juicy morsels. What I do believe is that those tasty mouthfuls of juicy morsels might one day turn into mouthfuls of sand before they start to spew them out.

Some of the victims have given up their ghosts, still brooding perhaps over the great agonies in their hearts. The majority of those yet living are still completely landless. So often I have seen the ever thinning figure of Jethro Kipergeng, our former assistant farm headman. I have heard that he is still squatting by the roadside; still waiting for some justice to happen which never seems to come. In turn, he has resorted in frustration to drowning his sorrows in illicit brews, perhaps waiting for the stock of his days on earth to run out, but it seems that his sorrows have on their own learned how to swim out of the liquor.I have also twice or about thrice bumped into Jackton Kipwarir, who is now a late septuagenarian and a dejected soul. He is ever talking to himself and soliloquises while walking alone, every now and again throwing up his hands and pointing at invisible beings. He also is still landless, squatting by the now disused railway line that used to lead to the prominent land of Katalel, although I have stopped seeing him of late and he seems to have moved to an unknown location. The rusty railway line ceased operating a decade ago and is now a lost glory of its former self. It is now bushy and bears overgrown bushes and it is hard to believe that it was once upon a time a vibrant and reliable transportation network.

However, there are others who have tried to the utmost of their abilities and bought themselves fragments of land so as to avoid being buried in the urban cemeteries or along river banks, still waiting for God to speak and secretly nursing the agony of their prayers which God seems to have failed to answer.

On the other hand, there are others who have borne the whole thing and went against the grain into prosperity, a thing which made me feel that we are not yet finished but have surmounted our former oppressors' intentions. Of late, I have had a series of encounters with some of our fellow victims who all together underwent those terrible experiences, which indicated to me that hope and determination are what make a human being accept the bitter past and move on. Whereas there are some who find it extremely hard to forgive and still harbour ill-will.

Recently I was cycling around Chesarma shopping centre where our fathers used to booze up in the evenings, when my eyes, just slightly ahead of me, caught sight of an aging couple walking abreast beside the road. The limping gait of the old man made me to recognize him instantly. It was the aging Arap Nyongio and his wife Tapwago.

I cycled at a moderate speed and slowly braked beside them, offering my hand to them. They stopped and offered their hands, both alike looking at me in surprise. At first, they seemed not have recognized me at all. After a brief introduction, they recalled me. They looked at each other chuckling and gave me in turn further prolonged handshakes, their faces beaming with smiles.

'I tell you! These days - kids hey! They ripen too fast,' Tapwago said giggling.

'They were just infants the other day but look at him now; he is already old enough to be a father,' she added as we all laughed.

'My son, I am happy to see that you have really grown into a man of substance. I wish those wicked animals were here to see you,' Arap Nyongio said meditatively with tear laden eyes.

'I think it is a high time that we forgive them and leave it to God,' I answered back.

'Forgive who, my son? I will go on cursing him day in day out till I see God lay His mighty hands on him. That so called Mr. Chelagat is a beast inside a human body. I will not rest till I see him and his children turn to ashes,' he swore, licking his right hand index finger and pointing it towards the sky.

'Your curses on him are like a hen's curses directed towards the eagle. In fact, the guy is gaining fame at every sunrise. I recently heard over the news that he has been promoted to be a Provincial Administrator and he is now the provincial head in charge of the Northern frontier,' I updated him.

'I do not care even if he becomes the head of state. He burnt our homes in a brutal and inhuman way. In my opinion, he wanted all of us dead. Up to this very moment, I have preserved the ashes I collected from my burnt house. I will only discard them when I hear that God has punished him,' he said, looking heavenwards, his body beginning to shake.

'It is enough Papa. Let's leave vengeance to God. I beg to leave,' I excused myself, slightly startled by the old man's utterances that were burdened with heavy bitterness.

'It is okay my son. Go well and pass our regards to your parents. Tell them we are still fighting on, waiting for God to give us eternal rest. We are in our sunset years you know,' Tapwago, who had been quiet for a while, said patting my hand.

'I will Mama,' I replied, extending my hand to Arap Nyongio who happened to be embroiled in his thoughts of the past, untold anger written all over his wrinkled face.

'Go well my son. Meeting you has been quite rejuvenating to us,' he said, patting my back.

I immediately mounted my bicycle and cycled away. After some distance, I looked over my shoulder and realized that they were still following me with their eyes. I waved cheerfully at them and they waved back with broad smiles. Deep in thought, I pedaled myself homewards without looking back. What astonished me was the depth of the bitterness the old man still harboured. Another shocking thing which I failed to understand was how a man could keep ashes for almost two decades?

Immediately I arrived at my house, I too was called on by unexpected visitors. I had just taken a seat when I heard the sound of a purring car outside. I swiftly rose towards the door. On opening it, my eyes met with the familiar faces of two young men with sprouting beards emerging from a black brand-new *Toyota Fortuner* car. It did not take me a second to recall them. They were my childhood friends, Kipsiya and Kipronyei.

'Hello Kipsisei, the meek and the prudent one,' Kipsiya said, reaching out for my hand.

'Hallo to you too, Kipsiya and Kipronyei, the rollicking characters of bygone days. What a surprise dudes! You have pulled a nice one on me this afternoon. It has been quite a long time since I saw you, brothers,' I replied as I ushered them in, all of us equally excited.

'Yeah, that is very true. Fifteen years I think. How has life been since our ways parted in those faraway days?' Kipronyei inquired as he took a seat.

'It has been all about ups and downs, flirts and starts,' I replied, rubbing my forehead.

I felt somewhat impressed when I learnt that Kipsiya had sailed against all odds and currently was a captain in the army. Kipronyei too was a budding athlete who had recently won two gold medals in two prestigious world indoor athletic championships.

'So we are not yet over. I am seeing that we are truly rising again,' I said thoughtfully as we broke into a chuckle.

'By the way, Kipsisei I have heard that you are a budding writer and a poet,' Kipronyei said curiously, with his usual charm that seemed not to have left him since those boyhood days.

'Not really, I am just a duckling dabbling in literary waters,' I replied, patting his head jestingly.

'Have you written anything about those miserable days? We all rely on you to make sure that all those terrible histories are written down in memory lane,' Kipsiya inquired enthusiastically.

'Not so much really, but just only a small poem,' I replied rising to my feet. I went to the drawer and fished out a piece of paper bearing a short poem which I had written a fortnight before, and handed over to Kipsiya who grasped it eagerly. The poem was about healing and it read as follows:

We are healing again
You mercilessly shattered our lives to pieces
With your horrifying destructive bulldozers
And with your bayonets you lacerated our hopes
But behold, we are healing again

You lustfully raped our virgin young lives
With your crooked sticks of manhood
Your whips dined on our semi-naked bodies
But behold, we are healing again
You constantly brought down our shelters

With your silently simmering metallic monsters
Exposing our nude bodies to be feasted on by mosquitoes
But behold, we are healing again.

You created roofless and wall-less houses for us
Exposing our tender heads to be sun-burned and scorched
As the rest of the world watched and jeered
But behold, we are healing again.

There you still reside in your ill-gotten sophistication
As their bonafide inhabitants continue to languish
But here I can still stand wide-mouthed to say
Behold, we are healing again.

By the time Kipsiya was through reading it, his eyes were already moist. He looked up, stifling welling tears.

'It is a nice one. We are truly healing again and nothing will stop us from moving on,' he uttered in a tearful tone, passing the paper over to Kipronyei, who too seemed to be dying to read it.

'Nothing will stop us from surging ahead!' I answered, feeling my eyes too beginning to well up with unshed tears, and I looked away.

After going through the poem, Kipronyei handed it back to me with a nod. 'You have tried, but we are in need of something weightier - a book would suit the purpose,' he said in a congratulatory tone.

'I will try that very soon brother,' I assured as he rose to hug me.

All of a sudden after taking his seat, I saw Kipronyei's eyes glued right on the wall as he tried to screw up his eyes to catch a clear view of something.

'Who does this photograph of men in uniforms hanging on the wall belong to?' he finally asked, rising to his feet to get closer view of it.

'Who do you think it is?' I asked him jestingly, trying to establish the photo he was inquiring about. He had by then been joined by Kipsiya, who too seemed to have an equal interest in it. They were staring at one of my many photos hanging on the wall. He was referring to one picture in which I was shown shaking hands with a Cabinet Secretary and one of the country's top security officials. The photo had been taken some years back when I was being commissioned into a member of the inspectorate in the police service.

'It is this idiot!' Kipronyei said, turning back to me in disbelief.

'Kipsisei! Do not tell me you joined the police force,' Kipronyei asked, looking right into my eyes.

'Is there anything wrong with it?' I questioned him, feigning firmness and shrugging my shoulders.

'So you at last chose to join them, the ones who made our lives miserable and unbearable. The ones, who tormented us, brought down our shelters, whipped our mothers and detained our fathers? No, I cannot believe this!' he uttered, eyeing me accusingly and with dismay, both of his hands on his head.

'Yes, I joined them, so what?' I blustered, slightly irritated by his accusatory tone.

'Okay, I can see they have already poisoned your mind. You have already got promoted and you will soon scale your career ladder one more steps upwards. This will then enable you to be issue unlawful orders to your juniors to go and inflict pain on the poor. You will be manipulated by men of greed, and used as a tool to attain their material desires. You will bring down widows' houses, flatten orphans' orchards, whip the hungry and expose innocent children to sun and rain. Yes you will Kipsisei; you will thrust the needy from the path and force all the poor of the land into hiding.'

'No! Enough of this barrage of accusation, Kipronyei! You can't tell me that that is all that brought you two here. And even if you think I would act like that, then you will be among the men of greed yourself. You have already won two gold medals in world indoor athletic championships, only a third more and you will be damn rich. You will have joined the company of Mr. Champion and you will too be championing the land-grabbing team. You will use your money to corrupt the ways of righteousness and pervert justice. You will be injecting bribes into the judiciary so that the poor get no justice,' I fumed back at him, trying to swallow a painful lump of anger which had formed in my throat.

Chapter Twenty

'Hey gents, enough of these ravings or I slap both of you now!' Kipsiya shot up from his seat threateningly.

'I fail to understand the root of all these squabbles. You are both misplacing that anger of the past, bringing it to the present and directing it towards the wrong persons. I am pretty sure that neither of you will do whatever you are accusing one another of. You both share a similar background and I surely know that neither of you will enter into partnership with the wicked to barter away humanity anymore. You won't be part of those who have chosen to disgrace this world, our beautiful home,' Kipsiya intervened further, on realizing how bitter we were.

'Okay it is over,' Kipronyei said, cooling down but still staring at me like a cockerel being restrained from a fight.

We both sunk back to our seats with big sighs. After a while we had cooled down and involved ourselves in a chat that mostly revolved around the whereabouts of our childhood friends. I told them about my encounter with Arap Nyongio and his wife Tapwago, and narrated to them what had transpired that afternoon.

'I do not blame the old man. Some people can sometimes be so cruel to you to the extent that you find it difficult to forgive them for the rest of your life.' These were the only words that Kipsiya managed to utter concerning the matter.

I was mesmerized and impressed to hear that the duo had acquired pieces of land and resettled their now aging parents, confirming my earlier assumptions that Kipwarir shanties had disappeared from the railway side in which they had been squatting until sometimes back when they had vanished.

In the long run, the pair excused themselves, promising to come back the following weekend when we would deliberate on the plans to trace our former mates and maybe plan a party to celebrate the reunion.

After seeing them off, I got back into the house bubbling with excitement, happy for my friends' achievements. I went back to my couch, grabbed the remote control and switched on the television. It was a few minutes past six in the evening. There were no interesting programmes in most of the channels. Most of them were showing Philippine soap operas. I went back to my books and busied myself with some poetry.

I had gone deep into the books when I was prompted to look back at the television, upon realizing that the programme that was running had been cut short. To my surprise, my eyes caught some breaking news alert that had popped up from the bottom of the screen, which read that a fatal plane crush had occurred in the northern part of the republic and it was feared that a senior civil servant had perished. This completely took me off the books, somewhat shocked by the developing story. After five minutes a

Chapter Twenty

prominent news anchor appeared on the screen with more elaborate news.

'Good evening, our dear esteemed viewers. The breaking news reaching us now is that a fatal military helicopter crush has occurred, and it has been confirmed that one senior government official has perished. Early reports indicate that the two pilots manning the aircraft parachuted themselves to safety and are in a stable condition. The only casualty who is believed to have perished in the crash is the Provincial Administrator in charge of the Northern frontier, Mr.Katwa Chelagat. Further reports indicate that the plane and the unfortunate occupant have been burnt beyond recognition. We will get back to you when we get more detailed reports. Meanwhile, we take this opportunity to send our heartfelt message of condolence to the relatives of the casualty.'

Utterly shocked beyond words, I found myself in a state of disbelief. I could not believe that the man we had talked about that very afternoon was no more. I leaned back in my seat as a myriad images started to crisscross my mind. My mind flew back to twenty years ago when the wails from women echoed in my head. I could see the farm women circling their heads and casting invisible abominations towards the burning homes, pronouncing mouthfuls of curses directed towards the then District Administrator. In my mind I could see the image of old Arap Nyongio kneeling and weeping before the remains of his charred abode, those words coming back, ringing eerily true.

Engulfed in all these memories, I felt a hot dam of tears break in my eyes. Burdened with untold grief, I found myself lying on the floor doubled up, weeping terribly, and my entire body shaking. Strangely enough, I wept for many hours for something which was more than the untimely death of Mr. Chelagat, but that strange taunting and haunting look that has been ever present in the eyes of my fellow victims.

Strictly speaking, there is one outstanding thing I have been noticing in the eyes of all the former victims with whom we underwent those terrible experiences. Ranging from all that I have ever bumped into, and those whom I used to be with, among them my friends Kipsiya and Kipronyei, our now departed Grandpa (God place his soul in eternal peace), my parents and my two elder siblings Kiptolo and Kilabat, I notice that they all have, or used to have, something *outré* in their eyes, common to all of them. There is something weird in those stolid dauntless eyes. Those tearless yet ever-crying eyes are always searching for something in common that can only be discerned by those who understand their past better. They are ever pleading and imploring to be given back that justice and human dignity that they were cruelly robbed of in the past.

To you, Bishop Felix Gemu, I must say that you were, and still and forever it seems that you will be, the only real human being with a true human heart that has ever existed under the sun, particularly in this current ignorant world, in which indifference predominates. The world where a tender and unseasoned girl is raped with a crooked stick of manhood right in the public eye, and a cripple is robbed of his walking aids and decapitated in broad daylight while the rest of the world sit back and watch. You were the first person in my life to mourn in so heartfelt a fashion; so much because you were the only one among the millions who stood out for us, who showed concern and shed tears over our sorrows and misery, only a few days later to be brought into a permanent state of silence by that fatal metallic embrace. You are one of the great who died a greater death, for you died with the better part of our smiles in your heart. Your blood, which hated injustice, was congealed within your own body; your breath which loved voicing the voices of the voiceless, was cast out of your lungs and your eyes that used to shed tears over the oppressed were forever shut to the world.

www.ingramcontent.com/pod-product-compliance
Lightning Source LLC
Chambersburg PA
CBHW071234080526
44587CB00013BA/1610